BIRDS
OF SOUTHERN ARABIA

**Written and photographed
by Dave Robinson
and Adrian Chapman**

Published with
the support and
encouragement of

MOTIVATE
PUBLISHING

Published by
Motivate Publishing

PO Box 2331
Dubai, UAE
Tel: 824060
Fax: 824336

PO Box 43072
Abu Dhabi, UAE
Tel: 311666
Fax: 311888

London House
26/40, Kensington High Street
London W8 4PF
Tel: 071 937 4024
Fax: 071 937 7293

Directors:
Obaid Humaid Al Tayer
Ian Fairservice

Senior Editor:
Julia Roles

Art Director:
Mark Pettipher

First published 1992

ISBN 1 873544 37 5

Printed by Emirates Printing Press, Dubai

CONTENTS

Front cover: A colourful Indian Roller, common amongst the mangroves and along the coastal towns of the Batinah Coast.

Back cover: A White Stork in flight.

Title page: Greater Flamingoes, the largest of the wading birds.

This page: A Red-billed Tropic-bird from the deep oceans which breeds in the Gulf. (Photo: Maarten Verhage)

INTRODUCTORY TOUR

Bright green parties of parakeets dashing across the city skyline, wheeling white sea-birds far out over the azure blue Gulf waters, the flicker of black and white wings by a desert track — that's about the extent of most people's knowledge of the birds in the Gulf. It may come as a pleasant surprise to learn that around 370 or so different species of birds have been seen in the UAE and neighbouring states. Of these, about 60 are known or thought to breed here, the remainder visit during seasonal movements or pass through on migration. In short, there is an amazingly varied and ever-changing bird population to see, and this book sets out to introduce them to you.

Our aim is to help you put a 'name' to that familiar — or unfamiliar— bird. With more than a little luck we have photographed not only the commoner species but a few of the more exotic varieties as well and hope that through our photographs, which illustrate the book, we have managed to capture enough of the beauty of these fascinating creatures.

Interest in natural history is a relatively recent phenomenon here and most of the current information has been gathered by a handful of enthusiasts over the past 40 years. For those with more than a cursory interest in the subject there are many exciting discoveries yet to be made and anyone who has a mind to, can contribute to the sparse knowledge of the region.

We have divided the book into chapters according to habitat. Habitats are surprisingly varied within the region; our bird-watching tour moves from the islands, through the gardens and deserts, to the mountain peaks. Being highly mobile creatures, birds can be found in a variety of habitats, particularly during migration periods. However, most birds have specialised in exploiting a particular habitat along with a specific food supply and amazingly wherever these conditions exist they usually manage to find them.

We hope you enjoy the book as much as we have enjoyed compiling it. We look forward to seeing you out in the field, binoculars in hand, discovering new species, noting range extensions, finding breeding sites or just being enthralled by the beauty of these creatures and the region.

A flock of Greater Flamingoes coming in to roost in the evening at Al Ghar lake, where up to 300 overwinter.

5

A resplendent male and a drab female (inset) Red-backed Shrike displaying the plumage variations common in many bird species.

ISLANDS AND HEADLANDS
migration outposts

We begin our bird-watching tour on an isolated rocky island surrounded, for as far as the eye can see, by the warm blue waters of the Gulf. An idyllic setting, but with only sparse vegetation and limited fresh water, at best, it is not a location you would expect to produce a great variety of birds; particularly birds associated with forests and fields or mountains and marshes, plush pastoral scenes full of greenery and running water. And yet, at certain times of the year, all types of birds can be found on these islands right in the middle of the Gulf. These times corrrespond to the migration seasons which occur twice a year. Since roughly 90 per cent of the region's birds are migrants, many different species can be found on these remote rocky islands during this period.

Traditionally, islands have been used to study bird migration. Islands are easy to reconnoitre, so arrivals and departures can be logged, almost like at an international airport. Isolated from the mainland, arriving birds are either migrants or visitors. Because migration has such a profound influence on birds and bird-watching in this region we begin by examining this phenomenon and some of the birds which undertake these flying visits.

There are two migration seasons. In spring, from March to May the birds fly from their ancestral homelands in Africa and south Asia and journey northwards through this region to breed. The summers of northern Europe and Asia provide plenty of food and shelter and less competition for the birds than if they were to stay at home. However, with harsh winters ahead, the birds and their offspring return in autumn, from August to October, when the abundance of food diminishes. During both these periods birds pass through the southern Gulf in unestimable numbers, certainly billions. Some actually stay longer and become winter or summer visitors or even residents, but these are birds we'll discuss elsewhere. The true migrants perform astounding feats of endurance, when you consider a small warbler, only 10 centimetres in length, which flies several thousand kilometres, twice a year, some from as far away as Siberia. They overfly the Gulf, deserts and mountain ranges. Most fly high and at night, so the great masses of birds go unseen. As a consequence the true picture of migration may never be known. However, it is not difficult to imagine how, when crossing the Gulf, this barren island could become such an attraction to tired birds or a temporary haven; and why, at particular times of the year a chance to visit an island is difficult to resist, if you are interested in the birds of this region.

Most bird migration occurs on a very wide front and it is not necessary to travel to an island to see these migrants — they can be found throughout the region. However, birds tend to concentrate on islands. Similar behaviour can be noted at an oasis in the desert, or on headlands and peninsulas along the coast: the first and last land falls. Getting to an

island in the Gulf is not a particularly easy task. Most are privately owned or involved in commercial ventures and all are inaccessible without a boat. Consequently, we are greatly indebted to a number of friends who have allowed us to visit 'their' islands.

In Europe the swallow heralds the beginning of spring and it's no different here. Although it is possible to see swallows at most times of the year they are most obvious during the migration periods — swooping across the sky on their ceaseless search for insects, which they take on the wing. Swallows and martins constitute a particular bird family and several different species can be found, often together. Swallows, with their blue backs, red throats and streamer-like tails, are quite distinctive. But even at a great distance it is easy, with practice, to differentiate between them and martins. Martins, of which both Sand and House Martins occur during migration, are smaller, squatter and have a more fluttering flight. House Martins are blue and white and have a very distinctive white rump. On the other hand, Sand Martins are brown with a noticeable band across the breast. There are also much smaller numbers of Red-rumped Swallows, which have a pale rump, similar to that of a House Martin. But they look and behave like the swallows they are.

A Swallow heralds the migration season (left) and a migrant Reed Warbler (right).

More migrant shrikes, a Lesser Grey (left) and a Woodchat Shrike (right).

The sighting of increasing numbers of any or all of these birds signifies that the migration season is underway. This is the highlight of a bird-watcher's year, for large numbers of birds, not seen since the previous season or missed altogether can now be expected.

Our favourite island is Dalma which can be reached by a daily ferry from Mugharraq, near Jebel Dhanna. It is a rocky outcrop about 40 kilometres offshore. These days the town of Dalma is a bustling port with roads and shops, and even a hotel. It is home to a fishing fleet which harvests the rich waters surrounding the island. Away from the town, on the tracks that encircle and criss-cross the central hills, it is still peaceful and that's where we go in search of our migrant visitors.

All areas of the world are noted for specific bird families and in the Middle East one of those featured families must be the shrikes. It was on a visit to Dalma that we saw large numbers of Red-backed Shrikes.

We were having a quick look in one of the many nursery tree plantations before going into the hills when we found a large flock of these beautifully plumaged birds. The males have a blue-grey head and a black mask, which gives these birds their menacing look. The backs and wings are reddish brown. It is also important to note their distinctive black tails with white sides and grey rump, to avoid possible confusion with other species. Shrikes are aggressive carnivores with strong hooked bills capable of tearing their prey apart. They hunt large insects and often small birds which they catch in a sudden swoop from a perch. As they usually sit upright on an exposed perch they are ideal photographic subjects, as well as easy to spot and observe.

The second shrike species seen that day turned out to be the female Red-backed Shrike. Like many other birds the females sport a far more subdued plumage. These birds were much duller overall and the breasts were covered in crescentic markings. In all other aspects though, they were identical and just as deadly to the insects on which they were feeding.

In that same plantation, next to the sea, we found a Lesser Grey Shrike. This is a black, white and grey bird and can only be confused with a Great Grey Shrike, a resident bird. The Lesser Grey has a large black mask covering the forehead, is of heavier build and always seems much tidier than its near relative. This single Lesser Grey Shrike amongst the flock of Red-backed Shrikes, sat on its branch and allowed us to approach it; the only one that ever did.

Birds which are grounded during these long migration journeys tend to be tired and disorientated. As a result they are often easier to approach than their 'street-wise' local cousins. We have often been surprised at our luck in photographing relatively rare birds compared with the effort needed to capture worthwhile images of common local species.

Another striking member of the shrike family is the Woodchat Shrike. It is easily recognisable with its rufous brown cap. The black wings and tail separate a white breast and back, producing an unmistakably pied appearance in flight. Like its predecessors these birds perch prominently and swoop at passing insects.

Leaving the plantation at the southern end of the island, we headed inland and into the central hills. The land is mostly barren with occasional small groups of trees, often only a single tree embedded in a small fertile niche. The hills are rounded and seem to portray a molten volcanic origin. Through the influence of the elements, crevices and ravines have been eroded into the hillsides and the surface layers are delicate and friable. At last we came to a substantial grove of trees in a hollow, surrounded only by bare hills. This location was teeming with

birds of all descriptions. It turned out that this fertile location is the local sewage dump, which explained the large fly population and of course the birds. With birds, unfortunately, the case is usually — the smellier the better. You don't see many birds at clinically clean swimming pools, but go to a sewage plant..!

Most of the birds were warblers, a varied group of small restless birds that are noted for being difficult to observe and identify. We can add to that last observation, the problems of photographing them. If you find a bird in a bush and experience extreme difficulty in getting a good clear view of it, you can be sure it's a warbler. These small birds are all the more amazing when you consider the distances they travel every year during migration.

The prettiest of this group has to be the Menetries' Warbler. The bird has a disproportionately long tail which it waves and flicks incessantly. It is almost as if it is sending semaphore messages to other members of the group. The male has a dark cap, encompassing a red-eye, white throat, grey back and a dark tail, edged in white. The underside is light and can be pink-coloured in the breeding season. The female is dull brown but fortunately possesses just as active a tail. These birds also tend

A male Menetries' Warbler in the typical tail-waving pose of this species.

to be noisy, producing a wide variety of 'churrs' and warbles, intermixed. They fly from bush to bush, working their way down the twigs searching for insects.

By contrast, one of the biggest of this family is the Barred Warbler, a name which aptly describes the barred undersides of adult birds. They are a substantial 15 centimetres — large for a warbler. Unlike most delicate warblers these birds have heavy bills and bodies. However, they are just as difficult to observe and tend to skulk in the depth of the bushes. If you do see them clearly you can notice their conspicuous yellow eyes. Our Barred Warbler stayed in a single bush, and we spent over half-an-hour trying to photograph it, without particularly successful results.

Still in the tree grove, we next saw bits of a real skulker, known in our youth as a nettle-creeper, because of its habit of staying in the undergrowth. This was a whitethroat, named after its prominent white throat. The males and females again differ, with the male having a nice grey head. The best means of identification is the combination of a white throat and, if you are fortunate enough to catch a glimpse, the rufous colouring on the wings. When seen clearly, the beauty of these birds is apparent, but even on Dalma with such a limited amount of foliage around, this family of birds is difficult to spot and many escape recognition.

An Upcher's Warbler which eases identification problems by ceaselessly moving its tail in a characteristic manner.

Also in that grove, were Lesser Whitethroats, Willow Warblers and Reed Warblers. One of this family, Upcher's Warbler, used to be regarded as a rarity. Over the past several years increasing numbers have been reported throughout the region. The bird is a drab brown and offers little to assist the would-be identifier in terms of recognisable plumage features. Its actions and structure certainly place it in the warbler family and, like the Menetries', it has a very active tail. This is proportionately long and broad at the base and is constantly swivelled from side to side and up and down, which facilitates identification. On Dalma the Upcher's Warblers were found in the young plantations, signalling their presence with their tails. Having got the hang of identifying this bird, we see it regularly during the migration period, even when hidden in a bush or ceaselessly on the move, like the rest of this family.

Before leaving Dalma, there is one very special bird we should mention, the Sooty Falcon. This falcon breeds on the island and arrives before the migration season, living high in the hills. You can find the bird by scanning the horizon for a suitably sized stone. To our surprise, quite a few of these turned out to be Sooty Falcons; needless to say, many remained stones! The birds are similar in shape

Endemic to Arabia, a Grey Hypocolius passing through Sir Bani Yas, showing an almost fur-like appearance.

A Sooty Falcon from Dalma Island.

A migrant Wryneck hiding amongst stones.

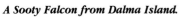
*A beautiful male Rock Thrush on migration
in the Musandam.*

Female (above) and male (below) Northern Wheatears, displaying striking plumage differences, common in wheatears.

to the Hobby, another migrant falcon. With their long pointed wings and long tails they are fast-flying attack machines. As the name suggests they are a uniform sooty grey in colour, with yellow feet and bills.

Nesting in the hills, they time their breeding activity so that their young can be fed on the returning summer migrants. This assures a healthy food supply for the young and adds yet another peril for the migrant bird. When we first arrived on Dalma we had no idea these rare falcons would be found here, let alone breed. Now it's difficult to think of Dalma without recalling them. Sitting among the hills in the late evening, having spent the day trying to separate warblers, we could see these Sooty Falcons rushing across the sky — the sun setting over the tranquil sea forming the perfect backdrop.

Another of our favourite 'islands' is on the mainland of Ras Al Khaimah, and is another magnet for migrating birds. Nestled between the high, rocky Hajar Mountains and the Gulf lies a thin fertile strip spotted with thorny acacia and mesquite bushes and the remains of old date palm plantations. Somewhere near Al Rams, for example, is a nice spot. This is another good gathering point for migrants at the other end of the southern Gulf.

Here, where the Gulf narrows down into the Strait of Hormuz, there tends to be a concentration of birds and we can see eagles regularly during migration, as these large birds have an aversion to crossing large expanses of water. All large birds of prey migrate by soaring up on thermals and then gliding as far as possible, while losing height. By endlessly repeating this routine they can cover enormous distances. Since there are no thermals over the sea, these birds can only cross relatively narrow expanses of water such as Hormuz, Bosphorus, Gibraltar etc. Big and powerful as these birds are, they cannot sustain energy-intensive wing-flapping flight over any significant distance.

Another well-represented bird family of this area are the wheatears, small thrush-like birds. Almost all of this family possess distinctive black and white tails of which the standard to compare all others to is the Northern Wheatear. The tail is white with an inverted black 'T'. The male of this migrant has a beautiful blue-grey back, shrike-like black mask and black wings. The female is a drabber brown bird but has the same tail pattern. They eat insects and are found on the ground or perched on small bushes. In their dashes for flies the tail is exposed providing instant family recognition.

By comparison, the male Black-eared Wheatear has a startling pied appearance and is not easily overlooked while on its perch. This is one of the few wheatears whose tail is not needed for family or species identification.

At the same time it is possible to see larger thrush-like birds, Rock Thrushes. The male of this family is resplendent with a blue-grey head and a bright red breast and tail. The female has a stippled breast and back. She possesses a nice red rump and red sides to the tail. This allows the female Rock Thrush to be differentiated from the similar Blue Rock Thrush of the mountain areas, a bird we'll talk about later. However, both Rock Thrushes have a very distinctive silhouette, being chubby birds with elongated heads, long bills and short tails.

In these areas the ground is littered with gravel, fallen leaves and pieces of wood. The trees are gnarled and fissured. This provides ideal camouflage for both wrynecks and nightjars, very specialised birds. Both have developed an amazingly effective cryptic camouflage, so much so that nightjars are rarely seen until they fly off from virtually under your feet. They rarely fly far and soon settle. We believe they then think they become invisible to mere mortals, often allowing a close approach. Whereupon, you see just how beautiful the bird is, with its spots and streaks and vermiculations of browns and blacks and whites. This theory however, only works when you are not carrying a camera, which obviously impairs their invisibility!

Nightjars are a sizeable 25 centimetres, they fly on silent pointed wings and have a unique profile and flight action. Even when you glimpse it from the corner of your eye, you know you've just seen a disappearing nightjar. The white wing patches and generally dark coloration confirms it is a European Nightjar. We do get a few of the rarer ginger-coloured Egyptian Nightjars though.

Nightjars are crepuscular or noctural — they are active in the evenings and at night, when they hunt insects in the air, like a large swallow. They have a small bill but an enormous mouth, for scooping up the flies. If you get close, albeit without a camera, you can see stiff bristles at the sides of the mouth, which also help in catching their prey.

The wryneck is similarly plumaged, just as camouflaged, and is usually found on the trunks or branches of trees. This 16-centimetre bird is a relative of the woodpecker family, the only one to be seen here, so far. These birds live on insects and berries and are occasionally seen on the ground.

The wryneck is also unique in that it is the only unprotected bird in the UAE. Why, what harm can this woodpecker do? Is it because trees are so precious in Arabia? No, it's due to a mix-up in the translation of its name. The bird that was supposed to be blacklisted was the cormorant, which has a serpentine or 'awry' neck, and is often cursed by fishermen. This is not an uncommon problem as frequently birds are given different names in different regions.

A Nightjar: the large eye and bristles around the bill are adaptations for catching insects at night.

To avoid this, scientists give animals, plants and birds two specific Latin names (which you will see in most bird guides.) The first name is the family name, and the second, the name of the particular species. Sometimes a third name is added which is a sub-species or variation of the originally identified species. In this way errors and duplications are avoided. For this reason the check list of UAE birds, at the back of this book contains both the local English name and the universal Latin name for the species.

So far we've introduced several bird families shrikes, warblers, nightjars etc. In our information we have provided not only descriptions of the plumage but where the bird is normally found and its main characteristics. Identifying a bird requires first placing the bird in a family. Bird families usually have distinctive behaviours and actions. For instance, warblers are small, active and difficult to observe; shrikes are prominently perched and make aerial sorties after insects. So by observing a bird's actions, its location, its shape, song, how it flies, the time of year etc., the bird-watcher can correctly identify a bird. It is not of paramount importance to have excellent vision. What is important is to learn how to observe birds — what to look for, and it's not only the plumage, the overall characteristics or 'jizz' provide the clue to solving identification puzzles.

Let's return offshore to another island which has proved particularly satisfying and rewarding for migratory bird observations — Sir Bani Yas. Lying just off Jebel Dhanna, it is another rocky island, similar to Dalma, Das, Zurku, Qarnein and Jebel Dhanna itself. With ghaf, acacia and mesquite plantations, orchards and decorative shrubs, small farms and fodder fields, it is attractive to birds and humans alike. Add to this the herds of free-roaming Arabian gazelle, rheem and impala racing through canyons ahead of your vehicle, and occasionally bird-watching is forgotten.

A second distraction includes the many imported birds, like free-flying African Crowned Cranes which do not yet appear on the bird-watcher's list of wild birds. However, special migrants are still seen. Fairly common during migration periods are the European Bee-eaters, and bee-eating they do, much to the dismay of bee-keepers.

These brightly coloured birds are typically in groups of a few up to several hundred and are normally heard before they are seen. On hearing their distinctive 'croop croop' call, search the sky for these delta-winged birds. They have a longish bill, very pointed wings, and a long tail from which the central tail feathers extend — a very diagnostic silhouette. When it lands, the colours on the bird come alive with red cap, black eye patches, yellow

A European Bee-eater which now breeds in Digdaga.

A Skylark, one of many lark species which can be found at the Al Wathba Camel Track.

chin and back, blue breast and blue and green wings and tail. It's difficult to believe just how colourful they are when you get your first good sighting of them. However, in spite of the brilliant colours, it's not the plumage by which the family is initially identified, but the actions and shape of the bird.

In recent years, the European Bee-eater has been found nesting in Ras Al Khaimah, in the fields near Digdaga. So this migrant may be changing its status and becoming a resident bird. The birds nest in holes excavated into a suitable sand face. While most birds will remain migrants it is interesting to note that birding patterns are constantly changing, ensuring that the hobby never becomes boring. However, honey production may be reduced in RAK as a result!

Back on Bani Yas, with its many cultivations, the bird life is rich and all the previous birds listed can be seen there. Even the Sooty Falcon occasionally flies over, possibly on a visit from Dalma. A rare bird which is unique to the Arabian Peninsula and nearby Iran, is the Grey Hypocolius. It is the only remaining member of its family (genus) and it is not really known what its evolutionary close relatives were. We found a single male of this species in one of the tree plantations. The male Hypocolius

is grey with black ear coverts and pinkish-buff undersides. About 23 centimetres long, it is similar in shape to a large bulbul. The feathers on the bird seem almost to resemble fur, which may help it as it spends most of its time in thick thorny bushes. We had never seen a hypocolius before, however, on returning to Dalma, a mixed flock of 22 were found in a single bush. The females in this party were plain brown and lacked the distinctive black ear-coverts.

We leave this fascinating island zoo of Sir Bani Yas to go to the Al Wathba Camel Track. The central area contained within the track has been cultivated to grow fodder, creating an island of grass within a sea of sabkha. Sabkha or saltflats are extremely inhospitable areas where nothing grows or lives. Al Wathba, which provides another good concentration point for migrants, is renowned in birding circles for its larks.

Larks are a large family of typical brown birds with many identification problems. They have a variety of bill shapes from pointed to conical, but as a family can be identified by their calls and flight,

Short-toed Larks are the commonest of the migrant lark flocks.

and are frequently seen on the ground. They are usually heavily built birds with a short tail, which accentuates their stoutness, and so stand out from other ground-dwelling birds such as pipits etc.

Compared to all our previous birds, with the possible exception of some of the warblers, they are difficult to identify, but not impossible — most times.

The rarest of this family that we've seen at Al Wathba is the Bimaculated Lark. Fortunately, this stocky 16-centimetre bird has a very distinctive black patch on each side of its breast. They are noticeably short-tailed, heavy billed and uncommon.

Both Short-toed and Lesser Short-toed Larks can be found, but Short-toed are the most common. From its overall appearance it can be identified as one or the other. For further definition you need a good look through the binoculars. They are similar to sparrows, with heavily streaked backs. The Short-toed Lark sometimes has a dull mark at the side of the breast. This seems to come and go depending on the actions of the bird, appearing particularly when the bird stretches its neck. The Lesser Short-toed has a markedly streaked band across the breast. The best means of distinction involves the relative length of the various feather groups in the wing.

Another migrant lark, often seen in winter, is the Skylark, a very familiar European bird, but a passage migrant here. They are usually, like most larks, found in groups. They are very streaked and possess a noticeable crest. Unfortunately we never see their dramatic song flights here so are again reduced to looking for plumage distinctions, once we are sure we're looking at a lark.

So having told you good eye sight is not important, we are now discussing minute feather details! Well, to really pursue this hobby you definitely need a pair of binoculars and sometimes a telescope, as birds, with good reason, distrust humans and rarely allow you to approach too close.

Previously, we were highlighting the need to observe not only the plumage, but the bird's actions as well, which are just as important for good identification. But you do need to look closely and carefully at similar-looking birds — remember most of these creatures are only 10-15 centimetres long, bill tip to the end of the tail.

There are many binoculars on the market. Most dedicated bird-watchers use a 10x40, roof prism design. Good ones are expensive. For the beginner or occasional user a pair of 8x30's is a good buy. What are these numbers, we hear you ask? The first number followed by an X is the magnification. Magnifications of 7x, 8x or 10x are suitable for birding. Below 7x there is insufficient magnification, above 10x the binoculars cannot be hand-held as we all shake — some more than others. So 10x is regarded as the practical upper limit.

The second number is the diameter of the objective lens in millimetres. This can be equated to weight and size, and therefore the stiffness of the neck after a long day's bird-watching. About 30-40 millimetres produces only a slight ache, at 50 millimetres and above a permanent stoop can result. Larger lenses produce brighter images but in the Gulf where the light is extremely bright, this is not too important. At this stage, we won't discuss the permanent disabilities which can occur through carrying a 600-millimetre telephoto lens on a suitably stout tripod!

Meanwhile, back in the migration season we've looked at a variety of birds and bird families, we've visited islands in the sea and the sabkha, visited the coastline and been suitably impressed by this remarkable phenomenon of migration undertaken by these creatures. Before leaving the subject, let's go to one last island, Qarnein, another rocky outpost with a unique bird: the Red-billed Tropic-bird.

These are white sea-birds with a body length of 50 centimetres, an equally long streamer tail, and a bright red bill. They do not pose identification problems. The Tropic-birds are superb fliers and dive for fish by making spectacular vertical plunges. A true sea-bird, its toes are webbed and legs short, making it ungainly on land. On Qarnein it nests in holes on the rocky cliffs. Unfortunately it is rarely seen near the mainland coast but is yet another special bird of these islands of the southern Gulf.

A pair of the rarer Lesser Short-toed Larks with the even rarer Bimaculated Lark (inset).

SEASHORE AND SHOALS
seabird sanctuaries

The title of the initial chapter on islands may have been considered a little misleading as we ended up at a camel track surrounded by a sea of sabkha. The point was that migration occurs on a very wide front, but islands, of any description, are a good location to look for concentrations of birds. Even our summer and winter visitors, and our residents, tend to wander off the beaten track, but mostly, should a suitable habitat exist, they will find it and there you stand a better chance of coming across particular species.

With sea-birds the same rules apply but to a greater degree. We've seen gulls in the desert, but only rarely. The true sea-birds tend to be found where they should be: at sea, on shoals and sand bars or on the shore.

The southern Gulf possesses all of the above, in abundance. Everyone has seen gulls along the corniche or off the major highways which run parallel to the coastline. This is one of the few observations made by the non-bird-watcher regarding birds in the region. But move offshore at the right time of the year and the sky becomes littered with white diving terns and wheeling gulls, the two major families of sea-birds to be found.

A speedboat-trip to the offshore islands lying just off the coast can be an exhilarating experience with the wind beating against your face as you are buffeted along.

These low-lying sandy islands form the last vestige of the coastal lowlands where they meet the sea between Ras Ghanada in the east, all along the coast, past and including Abu Dhabi, to Jebel Dhanna in the west. Some are mere sand shoals, their presence being dependent on the tide. Though most of these islands are salt flats covered by wind-blown sand, some are sandstone outcrops with low undercut cliff faces on the northern shore. Most are

A pair of Bar-tailed Godwits displaying their unique combination of bill shape and leg length.

devoid of vegetation but some are covered in saltbush and other similarly robust shrubs. On a hot day, devoid of shade, with the sun's relentless rays reflecting off the sand, the light is harsh and the birds waver in the heat haze. This is where many of the tern species breed in May and June — in a scrape in the sand or sometimes a small circular collection of shell fragments, totally exposed to the elements. As soon as the chicks hatch, they run off under the nearest piece of shade: a saltbush, flotsam on the beach or the overhang of the encircling cliff. While not our idea of home, birds breed here in remarkable numbers.

We had a rare opportunity to visit the three islands of Yasat, nestled between the Qatar peninsula and the UAE coastline. These islands have substantial amounts of saltbush and hares. We were amazed to see hares running off everytime we turned around. They were apparently introduced to the island and are doing well. We also found breeding Bridled, White-cheeked and Saunders' Little Tern.

A dark-plumaged Bridled Tern seen on Yasat Islands.

The Bridled Tern is a good species to begin with. They can be easily identified, as they have a dark sooty back. The white undersides often look blue, reflecting the colour of the Gulf, as they glide low over the water. The long pointed bill with a black eyestripe joining the dark crown is very distinctive.

As most of the other terns display a variety of white and grey plumages the Bridled Tern is very recognisable, once you have identified it as a tern. So what makes a tern a tern and not a gull?

A typical tern is smaller than a gull, has long pointed wings, webbed feet and generally a forked tail. They are sometimes known as 'Sea Swallows'. They are gregarious and, like the Bridled Terns of Yassat, are found in colonies. They are noisy, to the point of screaming, particularly if you are near their nest sites. Beautiful fliers, light on the wing with the grace of a swallow, they frequently hover and then dive for fish.

If you see a flock of birds and one by one they plunge out of the sky into the sea, you are looking at terns. If they are sooty-backed, you can be sure they are Bridled Tern.

A hovering White-cheeked Tern prepares for a headlong plunge into the sea.

Probably the commonest tern in these waters is the White-cheeked Tern. These can be seen off virtually any coast in summer and have a particularly coarse scream. In the breeding season their undersides turn grey so that the white cheeks stand out against their black caps. In all other respects they are a typical tern: narrow wings, forked tail and they dive into the sea. Usually seen in the same area is Saunders' Little Tern, the smallest of the region's terns. They seem to have faster wing beats and often appear virtually tailless. If this is not sufficient to identify them, look for the very distinctive, black leading edge of the wings.

On Murawah Island we found the king of terns, the Caspian Tern. Murawah is another sandy island where next to the fish traps on a sandbank stood this enormous red-billed tern. A sizeable 50 centimetres, larger than many gulls, this is a big bird and has an equally big stout bill to fit its frame. Black-capped and long-winged, it also plunges for fish. These birds can also be seen along the shores and the lagoons fringing the Gulf. Their size and the very obvious red bill aids recognition. The Crested or Swift Terns are next in size, but these are yellow-billed; followed by the Lesser Crested Tern, a mere 40 centimetres, with an orange bill. Neither of these birds are large enough to be mistaken for the Caspian.

The beauty of terns is more noticeable as you sit on a sand bar, near a nest site surrounded by the sea, and you witness a large mixed flock of terns screaming just above your head, diving for food, their chicks scuttling about your feet. It's an amazing spectacle put on daily by these 'Sea Swallows' during the breeding season.

On trips out to one of the islands, in Khor Dubai or while lying on the beach in Fujairah, looking out to sea at the terns with a telescope, a dark shape may appear but it's not a Bridled Tern. It is a sturdily built bird with superb flying skills, which you might find harrying the terns. These are skuas, the sea pirates of the bird world. They chase birds, usually terns, until they disgorge their food, they harass them in the air and steal their eggs and chicks on the ground. This description is enough to enable you to recognise skuas, the 'Sea Hawks' of the region.

They are passage migrants. Their dark plumage is brightened by white flashes at the wing joint. In ideal plumage their tails have elongated central tail feathers, although in our observations these are usually missing, having worn away. Both Arctic and Pomarine Skuas can be found here. Both have very variable plumages. The Pomarine is the heavier with a deep keel or prominent breastbone and of more ponderous build and actions.

Along the entire coastline and all the substantial islands, you will inevitably find a large bird of prey, the Osprey. These birds abound in this region and you will probably find them sitting on a post or a buoy or at their enormous nest sites. A unique family, separated from the rest of the birds of prey, the Osprey is at times mistakenly called the 'Fish Eagle'. A resident, it breeds on shores and islands.

Superficially resembling an eagle, its wings are long and angled, and it fishes in these waters by plunging feet first on to its prey. Upon catching a large fish, it holds it in its enormous talons, head forward, to reduce the wind resistance, and flies off to a nearby perch to consume its meal. Ospreys are well-known here and many of the nest sites are used year after year. The nests are huge circular tangles of twigs, flotsam and jetsam, below which the ground is littered with the skeletons of past meals.

The back is dark brown, but its head is light with a very distinctive band running from eye to neck. The undersides are light and there's a very characteristic dark comma-shaped mark at the wing or carpal joint. Common though the birds are, they make good bird-watching every time they are spotted.

Staying with resident breeding birds, one of the commonest here, but virtually unique to the Gulf, is the Socotra Cormorant. We've seen these in unestimable numbers, floating in groups so large and dense, they looked like a major oil spill.

A visit to a breeding colony between September and February, gives another idea as to their numbers. We went to Jazerat Sunayah, an island off Umm Al Quwain, in October. Most of the chicks had hatched. On stepping ashore we were assailed by the pungent smell of rotting fish, but with tens of thousands, possibly as many as a hundred thousand birds around, all requiring to be fed, it's what one would expect. The island, the shore and the surrounding sea was covered in cormorants.

Cormorants are large 75 to 80-centimetre birds, with dark oily-black plumage. They have a long dagger-like bill with a hooked tip for catching fish. A long awry neck (remember the poor wryneck) and a stiff tail. Using their webbed feet they swim underwater after fish. After a day's fishing, they run along the water to take-off and on reaching land, stand, wings spread out to dry in the sun.

Common along most shores is the Osprey, which uses its powerful talons to catch fish.

The Socotra Cormorant colony found at Jazerat Sunayab.

Two species can be found here, the commonest is the endemic Socotra Cormorant, which in adult plumage is dark feathered all over. We also get smaller numbers of Great Cormorants, slightly larger birds, during the winter months. These have a yellow bill and a white chin. The thighs also show white patches during the breeding season.

So far we've concentrated on offshore birds — those that eat fish — but on the shores of the Gulf and its islands, many birds can be seen running along the shore or wading into the shallow waters. This group of birds is called waders or, in American parlance, shorebirds. At the time of year that huge numbers of waders visit these shores to overwinter or pass through on migration, they are normally in their non-breeding plumage. This is a great pity since most of them have beautiful distinctive summer 'dress' — a pleasure to observe and an aid to identification. But our birds sport typically brown featureless plumage. None the less, with practice they can all be sorted out according to the huge variety of bill shapes, leg lengths and overall sizes. Each species has evolved to exploit its own ecological niche so that every piece of the shore and shallows can be probed for food. They can prove to be an identification nightmare initially, but each has its own characteristics or jizz, which often involves much more than feather patterns.

The largest of this family, around 55 centimetres, must be the Curlew, and then its smaller cousin the Whimbrel. Curlews can be seen at the shoreline or often inland along grassy embankments or road dividers. Their primary characteristic is their extremely long decurved bill which they use for probing the ground for invertebrates. The bill is so long it can be clearly seen in flight, when the bird emits its 'coo-loo' call from which its name is derived. Curlews are often found in small groups.

Confusion is only possible with Whimbrels, 40-centimetre versions of curlew. The Whimbrel's bill is heavier and proportionately considerably shorter than that of the the curlew. One way to judge bill length is to relate it to the size of the head. The Curlew's bill is always more than twice the head size, whereas the whimbrel's is a mere one-and-a-half times. Relative to the nose on a human's face, both are enormous — fortunately we don't have to probe the ground for our food. The Whimbrel also has a dark crown stripe and is known as the 'seven-note whistler', its flight call being a fast stream of seven or so whistled notes.

Similar in size, and found in the same locations, are the godwits. These 40-centimetre birds have long straight bills although a careful look at the commonest species, the Bar-tailed Godwit, reveals a slightly upturned bill. The Bar-tailed Godwit can be identified by its size and bill alone. In flight, the barred tail is shown and the lack of a bright white wing bar confirms it is not the rarer Black-tailed Godwit.

Another pair of shore birds are the Redshank and Greenshank. The names come from the colour of their legs. The Redshank is very common and its raucous 'chooee-chooee-chooee' call is always heard above all others on disturbing a flock of waders. The 28-centimetre Redshank has a straight red bill only slightly longer than its head. In flight the trailing edge of the wings show bright white wing bars. A redshank without the white wing bar could be a rare Spotted Redshank, a passage migrant.

The Greenshank is similarly sized and has an overall grey plumage. It is altogether a more delicate bird but not as common. The bill is slightly upturned, which is an important recognition feature. The call is a soft 'too-too-too'. In flight the bird shows a prominent white rump which ends in a point in the middle of the back.

So wader-watching and identification is easy so far. Waders abound in the Gulf along any shore, mud flat, creek or sand bar. Unfortunately they are often only seen in the distance, as silhouettes against the sea.

For this reason, body and bill shapes, calls which can be heard over long distances, and flight patterns are very important. These are one of the few occasions where binoculars are insufficient and we often use telescopes. We've found that a 20 or 25 x magnification is the optimum. Above this level the heat haze becomes excessive, and thoroughly distorts the image. Telescopes must be used with a tripod or, if in a car, on a window mount as the magnification is so high that they cannot be hand-held.

The state of tide has a profound influence on wader-watching, as they are usually found near the tide line. When you visit a shallow beach, such as off Dhubiyah or Khor Al Beidah, you will observe that if the tide is out, so are the waders, and all you can see are specks on the horizon. If the tide is in and there's no mud flat left, they go off to roost somewhere else. Get it right and you're guaranteed interesting viewing and an opportunity to test your powers of observation. However, if you take your swimming costume and a barbecue just in case, you're going to have a good day out anyway, along this often secluded and beautiful coastline.

There are a few other waders worthy of mention before we move on: the Oystercatcher in its black and white plumage with a long red bill and piercing 'peep-peep' call; the multicoloured Turntone that shows distinctive black and white patterns when in flight; the Dunlin and the Curlew Sandpiper.

The long-billed Whimbrel (top) and the even longer-billed Curlew (bottom).

*A delicately structured Greenshank seen reflecting in the
waters of the Dubai fish farm.*

In breeding plumage the last two birds are very distinctive, the black belly patch of the Dunlin contrasting with the red head, breast and belly of the Curlew Sandpiper. In winter these aids to identification do not exist. Both birds have decurved bills; that of the Curlew Sandpiper tends to be longer, and that's how its name came about. These are both sandpipers, around 20 centimetres in size, stockily built birds and renowned for their long distance migrations undertaken in huge flocks. The answer to identification lies in looking at the rump, which is white on the Curlew Sandpiper. Sounds easy enough, until you try it with the birds as mere spots on the shoreline, but persevere and you can separate all these species with practice. There comes a time when these brown birds do take on individual identities and it's satisfying to test your powers of observation and get the correct answer. We can guarantee a good test if you go wader-watching.

We've mentioned one special bird of the Gulf already, the Socotra Cormorant. The beautiful Crab Plover is another. This bird is the last remaining survivor, known as a relict species, of a group of birds which evolution has wiped off the face of the earth. Consequently, it now has a whole bird family to itself. Recently, a colony of these quite rare birds was rediscovered on the island of Abu Al Abyad, a large sandy island just off the coast, west of Abu Dhabi. For several reasons, the Crab Plover is unique amongst shore birds. Its black and white plumage, huge black beak and pale blue legs make identification obvious. Also, they nest in tunnels excavated in a sand mound, near the sea. The tunnels are about one-and-a-half metres long and as it is a colonial breeder, the nesting area becomes honeycombed with these tunnels, often several hundred in number. The bird lays a single egg which can be left to incubate in the sand, if the daytime temperature is sufficient. The young bird is born helpless, featherless and blind. All other wader chicks are covered in down and can walk or run soon after hatching. The chicks and the adults live almost exclusively on crabs, which the bird stabs with its great bill after a short dashing run. The young ones are dependent on the adults often right through to winter.

Although Abu Al Abyad is the only known breeding ground here, flocks of these beautiful birds can be seen along the coast. The mud flats around Umm Al Quwain or the Dhubiyah Peninsula are

Often confused with a Dunlin, this Curlew Sandpiper has longer legs, neck and bill.

Missing the light tip to this Sandwich Tern's bill can pose identification problems.

good places to look. Unfortunately, there seems to be good reason to believe that these very special birds are in serious decline in the Gulf. Because of their uniqueness — many of the local people remember these birds and recall large breeding flocks along the coastal islands — some form of extra protection seems necessary for the special Crab Plovers of the southern Gulf.

To visit the big Socotra Cormorant colony in Jazerat Sunayah we hire a fishing boat in Umm Al Quwain. This trip not only gets us to where we eventually want to be, but also offers ample opportunity for sea-bird spotting en route. In winter the sea can be cold and choppy and a drenching experience. In this area in winter you may find both Gull-billed and Sandwich Terns. These are medium-sized terns that can be easily misidentified.

The Gull-billed Tern, as the name suggests, is heavy billed and doesn't sport the normal long, straight, pointed tern bill. However, the Sandwich Tern has a light tip at the end of its black bill, but is similar in other plumage respects. Missing the

light tip of the Sandwich Tern appears to shorten the bill, resulting in a Gull-billed Tern's appearance.

As we mentioned earlier, gulls are much heavier than terns, with the exception of the Caspian Tern. Gulls tend to glide and soar in flight and never undertake death-defying plunges into the sea after fish. They are basically scavengers and often predators; they tend to be found in flocks and are frequently seen swimming or even sleeping on the water. They can be spotted along all the coastlines.

Several of this family are worth mentioning due to their scarcity elsewhere in the world. The Sooty Gull has dark brown upperparts; the belly and tail are white plumaged but the juveniles have a dark tail and white rump. It is only found between the Arabian Gulf and the Gulf of Suez. It always seems to have a long bill compared to its head and neck, making it look awkward.

The Great Black-headed Gull is a staggering 70 centimetres. The black head is only present during the breeding season. However, the size of the bird, the massive yellow bill, with a black ring near the

29

Very special to the Gulf are the Crab Plovers.

Great Black-headed Gulls at rest.

A Dunlin, for comparison with the Curlew Sandpiper seen on page 28.

An Arctic Skua in moult.

A rare Caspian Plover in breeding plumage.

tip, and the distinctive black and white patches at the wing tips make identification straight forward. The more sedate flight of the gulls, as opposed to the faster terns and dashing waders, makes them easier to identify in flight.

The Slender-billed Gull is also worth mentioning. These gulls have elongated heads and bills leading to the 'slender-billed' appearance. In the breeding season the breast becomes tinged pink.

Identification problems can exist between Slender-billed Gulls and visiting Black-headed Gulls, common throughout Eurasia. Like the Great Black-headed, these birds also lose their black heads in winter and resemble the Slender-billed Gull. Both of these species have very distinctive white leading edges to their wings, which can be seen in flight..... but which species are you seeing ? If you cannot make out the elongated head of the Slender-bill, look at the bird's attitude in flight; the Slender-bills are noticeably hump-backed.

Let's return to the seashore and look at another family of shorebirds, the plovers. We get lots here. All of this family are stout, short-billed shorebirds, usually seen running around the beaches.

The larger members of the family, the Lesser Golden and Grey Plovers are winter visitors, the former originating from eastern Siberia or western Alaska whilst the Grey Plover breeds on the high Arctic Tundra of Asia and America. In breeding plumage, which we see occasionally before they depart from the region, they are dressed in beautiful plumages, with black faces and undersides, and very patterned backs. The Lesser Golden is brown with golden highlights, and the Grey Plover is a mixture of blacks, greys and white. In winter that's not the case. From their size, upright stance and short bills they are very obviously large plovers, and in flight the Grey Plover shows distinctive black armpits or axillaries, making it easier to differentiate between the two.

The rest of this family are much smaller but have the same general silhouettes. There are Ringed, Little Ringed and Kentish Plovers. Both the Little Ringed and Kentish breed here. If you see a down-covered chick running off from virtually underfoot, it is in all probability a young plover. They nest in scrapes on the ground or on shingle beaches and are so good at camouflaging their eggs and young that you have to be very careful to avoid treading on them.

Kentish Plover (left) and Little Ringed Plover (right).

A group of Lesser Sand Plovers on the beach at Kalba.

Kentish Plovers are the most numerous and can be identified by their hunched-up running postures. In the breeding season the males have almost chestnut caps and incomplete black breast bands, separating them from Ringed and Little Ringed Plovers. The Ringed Plover can be set apart from the Little Ringed Plover by its white wing bar, bright red-orange legs and lack of an eye ring.

Birders often have difficulty differentiating between Greater and Lesser Sand Plovers. The Greater Sand Plover generally has a heavier bill, longer legs and is larger overall. This sort of distinction is valid when they are standing side by side, but this is rarely the case so the arguments will continue for a few years yet.

Two rare visitors are the Caspian Plover, which breeds near the Caspian Sea and the Dotterel of Eurasia and Alaska. We said most of our birds were well-travelled. Dotterel occur in small flocks and have been seen for a day or two resting at the camel track. However, only the occasional Caspian Plover is recorded. Our photograph is again from Wathba Camel Track and shows the beautiful markings on this bird. It is a long-winged, long-legged plover with a distinctive white eyebrow. Our bird was almost in breeding plumage showing a red breast, a rare sight indeed.

Well, in the main we've stuck to the coasts, all of which can provide good bird-watching along with eye strain and heat exhaustion on a hot day. But the choice of good weather and the right tides can make it a very enjoyable experience with lots of distractions for the whole family if the birds decide not to show up. Wader-watching certainly tests your powers of observation when trying to put names to distant silhouettes, but when you do get good views of these birds the drab browns come alive. On seeing these predominantly winter visitors you can only marvel at the distances they have travelled to enjoy the best part of the year here.

MANGROVES AND LAGOONS
naturally green retreats

Leaving the often harsh light of the beaches, little compares with the relief of entering the natural green shade afforded by the mangroves. In a land of blue sky and sea and yellow sand, the mangroves stand apart: as emeralds in a golden necklace. The combination of mangroves and lagoons suggests a richness of life unsurpassed along the coasts.

The mangrove is a unique plant with its thick green foliage supported by gnarled trunks and a web of roots, resistant to the sea and heat. Where few plants can survive, the mangroves impede the eroding power of the seas and create protected lagoons. They provide both shade and shelter. Within the intricate and often impenetrable root system a wealth of animal life lives and breeds. Small fishes swim in the sun-dappled shallow waters and crabs scuttle among the roots. The radial root system from which the vertical air-breathing shoots emerge stick out of the mud and make walking through the mangroves both difficult and often painful. Further out in the deeper lagoons large fish break the surface of the still waters and even the occasional Dugong can be found. Amidst the wealth of animal life, the birds have also exploited this natural green habitat.

Another odd yet pleasing thing about mangroves is that they seem to be relatively free of annoying flies. Wherever else you go in the region, as soon as you set out the picnic lunch, uninvited flies arrive, but within the mangroves you can enjoy a relatively bug-free break.

A great variety of birds is to be found here, each of them having evolved to occupy a niche in this rich environment. Along the shores and shallows, herons and egrets patiently stalk their prey. Ducks, geese and grebes swim in the sheltered lagoons while flamingos and spoonbills sift and sweep the sandy bottom. On the fringes, waders ceaselessly

Present in all the lagoons which fringe the Gulf: a pair of white phase Western Reef Herons search for fish.

35

A juvenile Greater Flamingo displays the neck and bill that make it immediately recognisable.

scurry and probe the mud for food and startling kingfishers streak by and dive after silver fish. Sitting in the shade of the mangroves all this and more is revealed if you are, like the heron, patient.

Easiest to locate but often difficult to get close to are the Greater Flamingoes and the white Spoonbills. Some 1.25 metres tall, the flamingoes are the largest of the wading birds. Their long legs and long neck allow them to occupy the deepest part of the water. Head down, they sift the water along the sandy sea bed to extract their food. They are ungainly looking birds and always a surprising sight in flight where they resemble partially opened umbrellas complete with handle. In the breeding season they are a lovely pink with much darker red and black wing panels. Social by nature they seem to work as a team when feeding. Up to a thousand can be seen in the Dubai Creek through the inevitable heat haze. They can be found along the southern Gulf in suitably shallow waters from Sila to Ras Al Khaimah.

Another bird adapted to life in the lagoon is the Spoonbill, with its remarkable bill which it sweeps from side to side while searching for crustaceans. The all-white plumage is set off by stocky black legs. These are also social birds and fly in regimented formations with necks outstretched.

Herons and egrets are next in size and can be found perched in the mangroves, stalking along the edges of the lagoons or out in the water fishing. They hunt their prey, either fishes or crustaceans, by cautious stalking and then make a final deadly lunge with their dagger-like bills.

Similarly sized to the Grey Heron is the Great White Egret. The size alone of this large White Egret sets it apart from Little Egrets nearby. On its own, it is best to look at its long neck, which seems to have been fabricated by a novice plumber from poorly fitted piping elbows. Herons and egrets use their long neck to advantage to search for and catch fish. They can sometimes be seen swaying their head from side to side, to get a better perspective of the fishes' location, before the inevitable fatal lunge — they are successful fishermen.

Western Reef Herons can also be found in the lagoons along with Little Egrets. Their running behaviour often seems at odds with their more usual stealthy approach to catching prey. They can often be seen prancing about with half open wings, and splashing like small children in the shallow open waters. In fact, this is another well honed ploy for catching fish. The dancing disturbs small fish and the open wings provide a large shadowed area on the water, improving visibility and increasing the chances of snapping up a meal. For some unexplained reason Western Reef Herons can have either blue or white plumages, known as phases, the blue phase being the most common. The white phase of the Western Reef Heron and the always-white Little Egret can result in identification problems, but you can separate these species by noting the colour and shape of the bill. The Little Egret's bill is always completely black and tapers gently to a fine point, like a stiletto blade. The bill of the Reef Heron is heavier and comes to a more abrupt point, like a dagger, at the danger end.

Smaller still and far more secretive is the Squacco Heron which fishes from the edge and cover of the mangroves. Patiently waiting in the shadows it grabs any unsuspecting fish, crab or insect that comes within striking range. Although drab-looking, it flies on bright white wings, which seem to appear from its otherwise tawny body. Similarly sized, the Little Green Heron is another resident of the mangroves but is more often found on the edges of lagoons, in coves or even harbours. It is less secretive than the Squacco Heron.

Further out in lagoons, ducks and geese paddle and grebes dive. Geese are basically larger, long-necked ducks but the Egyptian Goose seems to be the missing link and could easily have been labelled the Egyptian Duck. Introduced into the UAE they are showing up in many areas and are now found breeding in the wild. Quite large flocks of several hundred can be seen at Sir Bani Yas but usually only the odd pair occurs away from this original release point.

With their distinctive eye pattern and large black and white wing patches they are a most welcome addition to the birds found here.

Many of the following ducks can be found in the mangroves. Others have a distinct preference for fresh-water ponds but we have included them all in this chapter. Good fresh-water duck-ponds are to be found at the Zabeel Water Treatment Plant in Dubai, Hatta Reservoir and more recently the Al-Ghar Lake, in Abu Dhabi. For those with a stronger stomach or poor sense of smell, Ramtha Tip in Sharjah is another excellent bird-watching site.

Ducks can be divided into dabbling ducks and diving ducks. The dabblers often up-end, that is stretch down to pick vegetation from the bottom of the pond, pushing their tails up in the air. These

A Little Green Heron on the shore.

A more secretive Squacco Heron in the mangroves.

ducks jump into the air when taking flight. Typical of these are the Mallard, Shoveller, Teal, Garganey and Pintails.

Another duck, the Wigeon, grazes on grassy banks like geese, or picks up surface food. The diving ducks, on the other hand, feed underwater and run along the water surface before taking to the air. They are represented here by the Pochard, Ferruginous and Tufted Duck.

The largest and best-known duck is the Mallard. The drake is a beautiful bird in the breeding season with its dark green head, white collar and vinous brown breast. Like all ducks during the eclipse period it resembles the brown female. This is primarily to confuse bird-watchers — and predators!

During the eclipse period the moulting of feathers is often so severe as to make flight impossible. The ducks become very wary and secretive at this time, for obvious reasons.

Again, typical of ducks, the Mallard has a brightly coloured wing patch or speculum which in this case is blue and usually kept hidden in the folded wing. In flight or when stretching, this secret is revealed and certainly aids identification of this and all the other ducks.

The Shoveller is well-named after its enormous bill which is often used in a sweeping action during feeding. As a result it cannot hide its identity even during eclipse. In breeding plumage the male's green head, white breast and rufous belly enhance its appearance.

Small fast-flying ducks are either Teal or Garganey. In breeding plumage, both drakes are magnificent but very difficult to separate at other times of the year. The Teal has a striking almost mosaic-like head pattern of red and green, and a bright green speculum. The Garganey has a vivid white eye stripe and drooping wing quills. Separating the females and the eclipse males can be very difficult but is possible with practice.

The Pintail as the name suggests is long-tailed. This also disappears during the moult but the bird's long neck is readily identified, even in silhouette. The brown and white patterned face and neck make the breeding drake a beautiful bird to watch. Finally, the Wigeon has a cream forehead and crown and a distinctive head shape.

Of the diving ducks the Pochard is the most common example. The rufous head, black breast and grey body present an attractive picture.

A male and female Mallard showing contrasting breeding plumages.

A rarer Black-tailed as opposed to Bar-tailed Godwit.

In addition to ducks, grebes can be found in the area. These are true diving birds and use their skills to catch fish. They can be frustrating to watch and worse to photograph as they regularly disappear from sight for several minutes, only to pop up far away from where they originally submerged. You find them and they disappear again. Two species regularly found here are the Little Grebe or Dabchick and the Black-necked Grebe. The Little Grebe breeds in the area and is the smallest of the water birds. They have the habit of whinnying, almost like horses, across the surface of the pond. The Black-necked Grebe is a larger, longer necked bird with penetrating red eyes.

One last duck-like bird is the Coot, a fresh-water pond dweller. This black bird with its dramatic white forehead is often seen strenuously swimming with jerking head movements. As the feet are lobed and not webbed, extra effort is needed to cross the pond. The expression 'daft as a Coot' is derived from its quarrelsome nature leading to frequent squabbles.

These are some of the swimmers that can be seen on the lagoons and ponds. On a day when the still water is disturbed only by a brightly plumaged swimming drake, and this beautiful bird is reflected in the water, the combination makes a superb picture and excellent bird-watching. However, when seen in silhouette and eclipse plumage in the distance, birding can become very frustrating.

So having searched the water surface, several times, in pursuit of the frequently submerged grebes, it is time to explore the water's edge where the waders have been running to and fro. Again some of the birds described here have a definite preference for fresh water.

Among the larger birds can be Black-tailed Godwits, relatives of the Bar-tailed Godwit. In flight the large white wing bar and the black and white tail are obvious, but not when on the ground where it spends most of its time. The bird's long, very solid, almost straight bill is an important distinguishing feature but even that does not help when the bill is buried up to the hilt in mud, or the head is under water, as is often the case when it is feeding. Then the almost uniform body plumage aids the discerning birder to distinguish Black from Bar-tailed Godwits. What is important about the Godwit is that it uses its long legs and long bill to reach parts of the mud that other birds cannot.

Birders become very divided over wader-watching, and we are no exception. Many revel in resolving the identification problems which surround these birds; others avoid it, being content to label a few and leave the rest. Fortunately, in these locations there are sufficient varieties available for everyone, including the next wader.

A Kingfisher, perched and ready to spear a passing fish, displays electric blue back feathers.

Portrait of a Grey Heron.

A similarly sized Great White Egret.

A Little Grebe in breeding plumage.

A common Little Stint.

The much rarer Long-toed Stint.

The Black-winged Stilt is very well-named, with its black and white plumage and incredibly long legs. You normally find it feeding in relatively deep water where its distinctive pied appearance is clearly visible. If the bird should then come ashore, the legs appear to grow and grow until its body takes on diminutive proportions as it totters, precariously balanced upon these stilts. The bird breeds here, and there is no mistaking the chicks with their disproportionately long legs. These birds feed on insects picked from below or on the surface of the water. A less common relative is the equally pied Avocet with its long upturned bill.

At the opposite end of the scale to stilts are stints, the smallest of the wader species. By far the commonest is the Little Stint, a mere 15 centimetres. This wader is typically found at the water's edge, scurrying along and rapidly pecking near the shoreline in a continual feeding activity.

Even in winter the upper parts of this bird are well marked with light edges to the feathers. It also has short black legs and a short black bill.

By contrast, Temminck's Stint has much drabber and more uniform plumage and light yellow or green coloured legs. This stint is more often seen at inland fresh-water sites, and usually in small numbers.

The Little Stint on the other hand is usually found in much larger groups and is frequently seen along the coast as well as at fresh-water sites. Both of these birds breed in the far north and travel here for the winter.

Those used to be all the stints that had been recorded in this region until a Long-toed Stint was identified. Long-toed Stint have brighter plumage than Little Stint, the light legs of Temminck's Stint, as well as long legs and a long neck. These are still very rare in the region, but now that we know what to look for, no doubt more will be sighted.

Another extensive family of waders are the sandpipers of which Marsh, Common, Terek, Wood, Green and Broad-billed may be found. Quite a selection and a challenge to any aspiring bird-watcher.

The Marsh Sandpiper is mainly found in fresh water and could easily be renamed the 'Elegant' Sandpiper. The finely pointed bill and generally dainty structure give it a graceful appearance. It is usually found feeding out in the water, as deep as its legs allow, where it picks off surface insects.

The Terek Sandpiper on the other hand is a much more robust bird. The heavy upturned bill just doesn't seem to fit quite correctly. A single Terek attracted thousands of bird-watchers to northern England recently. Here in the UAE, they can always be found along the banks of the lagoons bustling back and forth in search of food, on short orange legs and head held low so that its bill is parallel to the ground.

All sandpipers bob occasionally but none more so than the Common Sandpiper. On close inspection, this dull-looking brown bird reveals beautifully fine vermiculations in the wings. These birds are rarely seen in the water as they prefer to search the shores for insects. In flight, white wing bars are exposed as it glides on bowed wings while whistling its shrill cry.

The Wood Sandpiper definitely prefers fresh water where it can usually be found near the water's edge. The spotted appearance of the body and distinctive light eye stripe aid identification. This is a relatively long-necked and long-legged bird. It can often be seen with Green Sandpipers whose darker back and very distinctive dark underwings help differentiate between these two similar species.

Groups of birds are usually called flocks, flights, or even congregations. However, many birds have specific group names like a sord of Mallards, a knob of Pochard or a spring of Teal. More fanciful collective nouns include a covert of Coot, an exaltation of Larks, a stand or wing of Plovers and a desert of Lapwing. Two other waders which have specific group names are referred to as a hill of Ruff and a walk or wisp of Snipe.

In the Ruff species of waders, the male and female, known as Ruff and Reeve, are of different sizes — 30 centimetres and 23 centimetres respectively. So when you first see them, it seems as if two species are present.

In their winter plumage the birds are best recognised by shape; they are very upright and have a heavy straight bill. The flight and back feathers are light-edged, giving a mottled effect, and the back feathers are often raised, no doubt to aid cooling. The legs are often red in colour.

The Snipe is yet another wader with a distinctive silhouette. They have an enormously long straight bill and very cryptic plumage. If they are disturbed they often fly off in a characteristic zig-zig fashion, initially close to the ground before gathering height or towering and then dropping back into hiding.

This Wood Sandpiper shows the spotted plumage and long neck which aid recognition of this species.

An extremely long-legged bird, the Black-winged Stilt.

A Ruff (above), feathers raised to aid cooling, and a Snipe (below) with its long straight bill.

Egyptian Geese from Sir Bani Yas which are now feral breeders.

Feeding among the mangroves, a Terek Sandpiper, a common winter visitor.

Seen throughout the Northern Emirates, this colourful Indian Roller is at home in the mangroves.

Both of these bird species can be found in freshwater pools or even wet fodder fields or gardens.

After all these brown birds you definitely feel like putting a bit of colour into your bird-watching — well this is the right area. Common amongst the mangroves and along the coastal towns of the Batinah Coast is the spectacular Indian Roller. Even more rewarding is its habit of perching in prominent locations while waiting for a large insect to pass by. On the perch with its heavy black bill, chestnut head and breast this Roller shows some bright blue in the wing. When it launches into a glide to catch its prey the beautifully plumaged bright blue, purple and black wings and tail are exposed in an explosion of colours. With their coarse clattering calls they certainly relieve the monotony of brown bird-watching.

Still sitting in the shaded mangroves a bright blue flash darts low and fast over the lagoon, accompanied by a shrill 'chickee - chickee' call. That was a European Kingfisher telling all in the vicinity that it possesses the sole fishing rights to this stretch of water. These legendary birds with their electric blue or green backs, changing colour with the angle of the sun, are not uncommon in the mangroves throughout the winter. Unfortunately, they rarely sit and dive for fish right in front of you. On the occasions that they do, you can only marvel at the enormous heavy bill, red belly, blue wings and shiny blue back.

It is not surprising they are named the kingfisher or occupy such prominence in bird books and pictures. Although, on seeing a kingfisher flash by for the first time, most people are surprised at how small they are — a mere 16 centimetres.

If you venture into the Khor Kalba mangroves you stand a very good chance of seeing a larger kingfisher, a White-collared Kingfisher. These heavy-billed birds sit adorned in their turquoise and white finery on a fishing perch in the mangroves. Although distinctively coloured they are rarely seen until they move, further away of course.

The unique population of this Indian bird breed only in the Khor Kalba mangrove and at least 25 have been seen. How they got here and why they have not spread to other similar mangroves, we don't know. There is a similar isolated population on the Red Sea coast, and these are the only known breeding areas throughout the whole of Arabia.

Amongst the rubbish of Ramtha Tip it's possible to see a third species of this family, the Pied Kingfisher which occasionally overwinters here. These large 25-centimetre birds have the habit of hovering prior to plunging after fish.

On leaving the shade of the mangrove at the end of the day, the maniacal cackling from deep in the foliage eventually ceases. This has been going on all day and occasionally glimpses of a brown bird are seen. It rarely shows itself and may alight briefly on the mud to pick up a crab. These are aptly named Clamorous Reed Warblers and they don't pose for photographs. Their loud calls tell you you're in the mangroves with their own special kinds of birds; naturally green retreats along an often stark coastline.

Found only in the mangroves of Khor Kalba, the large White-collared Kingfisher has established a breeding population.

*A male Black Redstart of the Middle East race
sitting amid colourful bougainvillaea bracts.*

PARKS AND GARDENS
outdoor aviaries

Prior to arriving in the Middle East for the first time, one conjures up visions of drifting desert sands of various shades of yellow, relieved only by the occasional palm tree. However, upon arrival it's not the high-rise buildings of glass and concrete and the wide boulevards that impress, it's the amount and the variety of greenery. Beautiful flower displays at roundabouts, central road dividers complete with mature trees (and not only palms) grassy embankments, decorative fountains — and that's only on the drive from the airport!

Later you discover that all the cities have large parks and gardens and even woods. Not at all as envisaged. To a birder, newly arrived in the region, the sight of so much greenery suggests a host of birds. Then a flock of fast-flying green birds squawks loudly overhead, a mynah cackles from a lamp-post and familiar House Sparrows chirp in the nearby bushes. After getting the immediate priorities sorted out it's time to get the binoculars out of the suitcase to explore the environs properly. Soon you realise you're in a large outdoor aviary.

In a new area it's important to sort out the common species first, as only then will you begin to see and focus on the others. Also, what's common in one place is not necessarily common elsewhere, like those green squawking birds, for example.

Bird-watchers are not happy people until a bird has been named. The correct identification of a bird is very satisfying and provides the key to the bird's secrets. You want to know about its habits and habitat, whether it's rare, where it breeds, what it eats and to discuss it with fellow enthusiasts, none of which is possible without a name. In the field you subsequently learn to identify it when it is flying, sitting, feeding or when it is hidden behind a tree; this last feat being undertaken by only very experienced birders about whom legends are written and after whom birds are named. Armed with a name you can read all the available literature, agreeing or disagreeing with the authors' views. Most bird-watchers are apt to disagree to some extent; it's a characteristic trait.

Then like birds you look for a mate. It's much more enjoyable to explore new areas that way and it avoids many pitfalls, permitting discussions and arguments to be pursued in the field. In a small party with those extra pairs of eyes you inevitably see more birds. Unfortunately, on mass outings you tend to see less, as all those bird-watchers trampling through the bushes frighten these timid creatures away, leaving only the bird-watchers behind.

So right in the heart of the city we have the habitat, the birds, and a desire to put names to the commoner species; now we can begin to find out what else is hiding there, awaiting discovery.

The green squawking birds are Rose-ringed Parakeets, 'Rose-ringed' because when you get close the birds have black collars! However, at arm's length (be sure to have your ear plugs fitted) you will notice a faint rose pink half collar at the back of the neck on adult males. So how do you identify them when they are perched in high trees or flying over the city? Easy, they are almost the only fast-flying, green, long-pointed-tailed squawking birds you will see out here. Well, almost only, because there are a few larger ones around with red wing patches called Alexandrine Parakeets.

Parakeets, which are medium-sized parrots, are always found flying or feeding in groups, being very sociable birds. They have a large red, hooked bill and use this formidable weapon to crack sunflower seeds and tear into dates and similar food. The large seed pods of the acacia tree seem to be very popular. The birds were possibly introduced to this area but have since established residence in most of the coastal cities and are occasionally seen in the desert regions. They now breed successfully in the wild, based on the numbers seen commuting between the communal roosts. The observation of visiting parakeets both in the oil camps of the western desert in Abu Dhabi and at offshore islands suggests a tendency for these birds to migrate. If this is the case, they may have occurred naturally in the region, even before so many were introduced.

Another noisy communal rooster is the Common Mynah which may also be another introduced species. In Abu Dhabi they roost in the mangroves in the reserve beyond the eastern lagoon. In the hour before sunset they arrive in their hundreds to perch on rooftops, TV aerials and trees. When they've discussed the day's events, they fly off to roost in the mangroves. The squawking can still be heard as they fly around in groups, settle, then erupt again. As darkness falls the cacophony dies and the discussion is over for another day. This fascinating spectacle is repeated each evening for anyone wanting to watch.

Common in most towns are noisy flocks of Rose-ringed Parakeets.

Mynahs are closely related to Starlings and at certain times of the year we've seen up to eight different species in Abu Dhabi. The cackling Common Mynah is by far the most numerous. During the day they can be found strutting around, feeding in the central reservations and the gardens. They are yellow-billed, with the yellow extending around the eye in an orbital patch. The head is black and the body dark brown. They also show a large white wing patch in flight and are noisy, gregarious birds. They breed on ledges and holes in the city's buildings; ornate facades are very popular.

Above: A strutting Common Mynah

Amongst the several hundred Common Mynahs are a few Bank Mynahs. These birds breed in holes burrowed in bank sides, from which their name is derived. From time to time nesting colonies have been established within Abu Dhabi, Dubai and Ras Al Khaimah. Strangely, these colonies seem to disappear and reappear in an uncoordinated way, and this remains a puzzle. In appearance Bank Mynahs differ from Common Mynahs in that they are darker grey in appearance, have cream wing patches, red skin around the eyes and small crests at the base of the bill. During the day they can be found amongst the feeding mynah hordes.

During the migration season large flocks of Starlings arrive in their sleek speckled plumage, together with an occasional Rose-coloured Starling. Seen in adult plumage these latter birds are magnificent, with a beautiful pink waistcoat draped over their Starling frames. The young birds are a drab featureless brown and need careful attention to avoid being overlooked, or misidentified.

Above: A male House Sparrow, complete with bib.
Below: The drab female can pose identification problems.

Other species seen in the region, are thought to be escaped cage birds, but some increases in numbers suggest certain species may be setting up residence here. These include Superb Starlings from Africa and Jungle Mynahs, Asian Pied Starlings and Hill Mynahs from Asia.

Upon entering the parks you may be met with the ceaseless chirping of House Sparrows which most people are familiar with. The male with its black bib, grey head and streaked back is still an attractive bird when seen in good light, whereas the female needs a little more attention to start with. Both have stout bills for eating seeds.

In Bateen Wood, Abu Dhabi, which we visit regularly, we always know when there is a Sparrowhawk around as you are met with silence as opposed to the normal chatter as you enter. In western Europe, House Sparrows nest under the eaves of roofs. However, here they tend to make large untidy balls of dry grass in the tops of bushes,

Isabelline Shrikes are found in a variety of plumages but are always red-tailed.

Less common are the beautiful Masked Shrikes of the parks and gardens.

*The pleasant song of the White-cheeked Bulbul brightens up
many a garden throughout the Gulf.*

A female Redstart quivers her tail from her perch awaiting a passing insect.

seen in almost all the woods and plantations. It is worth having a good look at the sparrows, as both Tree and Spanish Sparrows have been found in the area.

Moving further into a wood you often hear a very pleasant call which seems to beckon you on with musical 'come-to-me, come-to-me' directions. These are White-cheeked Bulbuls, another introduced species from the Indian subcontinent. As the name suggests they have large white cheek patches, which stand out from the otherwise black head, and a bright yellow vent patch under the tail. These are friendly birds and can be found around human habitation. We have often seen them sitting on cars looking at themselves in the wing mirrors and calling to their own reflections.

There are also Red-vented Bulbuls, and now just about any other colour in between since they seem to interbreed quite readily. Individual birds often portray a variety of characteristics of each of these species. It is usually considered that distinct species will not interbreed or when they do the offspring are not fertile and will not be able to continue the line. However, that does not seem to be the case

here as the number of hybrids appears to be continuously on the increase.

A common migratory species is the usually silent Isabelline Shrike, a member of the family often known as 'butcher' birds, because of their habit of impaling their victims on the spikes of trees. The name Isabelline describes the plain pinky brown colour of the plumage. Again, just to complicate matters, a variety of sub-species exists in which the plumage varies from dull grey through rich browns to sandy shades. Fortunately, all of these sub-species have rich red-brown tails and this is by far the best identification feature. Most adult birds have black, broad eye stripes, resembling robbers' masks, which, along with the hooked bill, give the bird its menacing appearance.

They can be seen sitting upright on exposed perches waiting for a suitably tasty insect to pass by. Whereupon they swoop down on it, either in the air or on the ground and return to the perch to dine or impale it on a suitable spike in the larder.

Shrikes are particularly well-represented in the Middle East while still relatively uncommon over much of western Europe. If you are lucky you may come across the most attractive shrike, the Masked Shrike. A few of this species are seen during migration periods each year. This bird is predominantly black and white with the black creating a masked effect across the eyes. It is slimmer than the rest of this family and its appearance is enhanced by rufous flanks and light underparts.

Within the woods, during the migration season, large numbers of Spotted Flycatchers can be found. Superficially similar to the shrikes, these birds perch prominently and conduct short sorties to attack passing insects, frequently returning to the same perch. Considerably smaller than shrikes, these birds hawk smaller insects, particularly flies.

The birds are grey-brown with streaked breasts and caps. The name Spotted Flycatcher is derived from their juvenile stage, when they are very spotted. However, the Latin name, Muscicapa striata, correctly signifies their streaked appearance. In order to correctly identify these birds it is important to look at their structure and behaviour. They are best identified by their actions and structure (often termed 'jizz') rather than by plumage. It's an important step in bird-watching to be able to identify birds by behaviour and this example is a good stepping stone to achieving that end.

We find two other migratory flycatchers in this region, Red-breasted and Semi-collared Flycatchers. Both behave like flycatchers. Whereas the male Semi-collared is black and white, the female is brown but the large white wing patches distinguish them from Spotted Flycatchers. Red-breasted Flycatchers are smaller, busier birds with distinctive white markings on the tail.

In the shadier areas of the woods we may come across a pair of birds with bobbing heads and quivering tails. A bird showing these characteristics is either a Redstart or more often a Black Redstart. The name comes from their beautifully coloured rufous tails, which are best seen when they fly off, usually behind the next tree. Bird-watching in woods can be very frustrating.

Spotted Flycatchers are best recognised by 'jizz'.

The handsome male Redstart has a blue-grey back and sports a black bib and a rufous breast. In many descriptions the Redstart is often differentiated by its white eyebrow. However, the much larger black bib which reaches down to the breast, and the complete rufous undersides of the Middle Eastern Black Redstart are just as valid separation features.

Separating the females is not so easy but the Black Redstart is noticeably darker overall. This sort of comparison is fine but you are unlikely to see both species together. The quivering tail and flycatcher behaviour certainly add up to a Redstart species.

Other woodland birds are the Chiffchaff and Willow Warbler. Much has been written about these small warblers to help bird-watchers differentiate between the two. Most guides state they can only safely be separated by song, but they rarely sing during migration and both varieties occur here. However, only Chiffchaffs spend the winter here.

Most warblers are difficult to identify because they never stay still, and this constant movement is a distinct family trait. They are always busy, ceaselessly searching the trees for insects. They are very common during migration and work in parties, communicating with their soft 'hweet' calls to one another while managing to keep out of sight.

Portrait of a male Marsh Harrier.

If you really want to separate them, those that constantly flick their wings and tails are usually Chiffchaffs. Those with light coloured legs are Willow Warblers.

In gardens, open parks or other large grassy areas, where there may be a few isolated trees, you can see a lot further and the variety of birds increases, if you are early. If you're late at the weekends the parks will be full of picnickers and all the birds will be keeping a low profile.

Found in both woods and the trees of gardens, is a medium-sized bird with bright yellow and black plumage, that is ridiculously difficult to spot. These are male Golden Orioles; the females are a more subdued yellowish green with streaked buff breasts. These orioles can be seen in large numbers or missed entirely during the migration season and as birders we are frequently asked what that flash of gold was. Their ability to disappear in green trees is remarkable. We found two of these birds in a small copse but the passage of a Marsh Harrier overhead startled another six into flight!

A bird occasionally seen snipping away at the grass is a very large, long-necked duck, a Greylag Goose. It always seems surprising to find these in parks. The Greylag is the ancestor of the farmyard goose and several are reported each year flying through the area.

White Wagtails are one of the commonest winter visitors.

Blue-headed Yellow Wagtails, one of many sub-species.

Another bird you may happen to come across is the Glossy Ibis, a dark bird with an enormous long decurved bill which is so prominent that it can easily be seen even in flight. This bird's plumage is always glossy, usually seen as a bronzed sheen. During the winter, white egrets are found in reasonable numbers feeding in the parks and even the central road reservations. The relatively short yellow bill, heavy jowls and hunched appearance indicate that these are Cattle Egrets. These identification features are important due to the lack of cattle or water buffaloes in the area. In the breeding season the birds develop buff crowns and breasts. They also roost in the mangroves and tend to remain in a group, rarely being seen alone.

Where there are large expanses of grass, wagtails and pipits can be seen picking their way through the blades. Wagtails, as their name implies, have disproportionately long tails which they wag frequently. During the winter months a huge number of White Wagtails can be found. Their grey and black and white plumage patterns are very prominent as they wander about, wagging their tails.

The Yellow Wagtail is interesting in that it comes in more varieties, or sub-species, than any other bird. We mainly see Blue-headed and Black-headed Yellow Wagtails in the southern Gulf, but several other types do occur. In breeding plumage these birds are very colourful and pleasant to watch as they stalk through the grass in large groups.

It is also possible to find limited numbers of Citrine Wagtails within these areas. The Citrine Wagtail is basically a Yellow Wagtail with a distinctive grey back and noticeable white wing bars.

The buff colours on this Cattle Egret occur during breeding.

Still in grassy areas, you can see pipits wandering around, often alongside wagtails, to which they are closely related. They are brown, streaked, terrestrial birds with shorter tails than wagtails and a slightly more horizontal stance than similarly marked, heavier bodied larks. Like the wagtails they hunt insects in the grass. The most common species to be found in the parks are Tree Pipits who announce their presence with their 'treez' call. Pipits are tricky birds to identify at the best of times and all beginners have real trouble with this bird family.

However, the Water Pipit is the only pipit with dark legs and so is easily distinguished if you can get close enough. It's a much duller bird than the Tree Pipit and has a prominent eye stripe. The least streaked pipit is the larger than normal Tawny Pipit, a massive 16.5 centimetres compared to the mere 14.5 centimetres of the Tree Pipit. Although two centimetres may not seem very much it is very noticeable in the field and an important identification feature.

At the other end of the streaking scale is the Red-throated Pipit, which is boldly streaked above and below. In spring, just before it migrates it is sometimes possible to see the bird's red throat but normally it is the streaking that provides the key to identification of this species.

Completing this garden tour is a seagull, the Black-headed Gull. It is not uncommon to find large numbers in gardens. In breeding plumage the dark chocolate head is easily recognised but in winter this is reduced to an indistinct spot behind the eye. As luck would have it, they disappear northwards to the breeding grounds just as they start to develop into their summer plumage.

In the East Coast towns in particular, there are large numbers of Indian House Crows. These are truly urban birds and are never seen outside areas of human habitation where they scavenge most of their food. These birds have grey heads and upper breasts unlike the all dark Brown-necked Ravens of the desert regions. They are usually found perched on lamp-posts, TV aerials or telephone wires during the day, but seem to like palm trees for their mid-afternoon siestas.

The parks, gardens and woods provide an excellent habitat for watching birds and are conveniently situated in all the large cities and towns. The smallest grassy patch can turn up a surprising number of birds. In our short tour we have only touched on a few of the species that can be seen. Almost all the birds featured in the next chapter — Cultivations — also inhabit these areas.

The relatively large and drab Tawny Pipit.

A smaller and more colourful Red-throated Pipit.

A shining male Purple Sunbird in a Calotropis or Sodom's Apple bush, which few other birds inhabit.

CULTIVATIONS
growing reserves

The massive amount of planting that is going on in the region deserves special mention. In a world echoing with constant cries of doom from conservationists, the 'greenification' programmes moving ahead so rapidly throughout this region are exemplary. New forests of ghaf, acacia, mesquite, prosopis and tamerisk; massive fodder fields; vegetable and fruit farms; and even road dividers are providing a green patchwork crossing the deserts and offering more and more attractive habitats for birds, both resident and migrant. It may even persuade some migrants to stay on permanently.

It is often said by old timers that there never used to be any birds in these regions. This may be partly correct as in the past migrating species would have flown through the area without stopping.

The recent changes in the local environment — the provision of large scale shelter from the elements, food from numerous new plants, the inevitable increase in the insect population, and most importantly the availability of fresh water — have significantly contributed in attracting birds passing through the region to these areas. If these 'greenification' projects can be sustained, the number and variety of birds should continue to increase.

We have watched over a period of two years, the progress of common House Sparrows along the UAE coast road from Abu Dhabi to Jebel Dhanna — a stretch of about 250 kilometres. Sparrowless petrol stations and cafés one year are full of chirping, breeding sparrows the next. Similar population expansions have been noted with Indian Silverbills and Crested Larks. All of this is occurring in a very short time frame, more or less on a par with the developing greenery.

Birds no longer have to fly across empty desert tracts; just like the early aviators, they can follow the roads and the cultivations which now abound on either side and can even fly via the central reservations.

We gladly dedicate this chapter to those birds with the pioneering spirit needed to colonise new cultivations and of course to the people who are creating and maintaining them.

As well as sparrows, among the best colonists are the doves. Doves and pigeons belong to the same bird family. Through convention a large dove is a pigeon and a small pigeon is usually tagged as a dove. Of these the ubiquitous Palm Dove is easily the leader in the colonisation stakes. Elsewhere this bird is known as the Laughing Dove because of its chuckling call and possibly because there are few palm trees in western Europe.

Common though the bird may be, in the breeding season it looks very pretty with its speckled gorget or upper breast, and colouring of subtle browns and 'dove' grey. At only 27 centimetres, it is the smallest dove found here and needs to be identified quickly — otherwise you will spend half your bird-watching time checking them and missing out on the other rarer species. Typical of doves, it has a fast direct flight with rapid beats of its pointed wings, except when it is showing off by 'towering' or

gliding. The relatively small size, the bird's squeaky sounding wings as it takes off close by, grey secondaries and dark primaries, and white tips to the tail sides, all help you to recognise it.

The nests of doves and pigeons consist of a small platform of twigs into which two white eggs are laid. Usually, these are found in bushes — we've never found any in palm trees. But any ledge seems to do. The squabs or young grow quickly and soon fill the frail nest. Usually only one of the chicks survives; perhaps one falls out of the overcrowded small nest. However, this is not the explanation given in bird literature where lack of food is stated as the reason for poor survival. None the less, success in breeding is apparent as you find Palm Doves everywhere.

There are two other doves to be found in these areas, the Turtle Dove and the Collared Dove. The Turtle Dove is a beautiful bird and has scalloped turtle-shell-like feathers on the wings and back. The dark centres and light sandy-coloured edges of these feathers produce this attractive pattern. On the sides of the neck the adult birds show a chequered black and white patch.

We don't see Turtle Doves all year round but they do appear in the summer, which is surprising as most birds — and people for that matter —

A common, yet pretty, laughing Palm Dove.

A species which is increasing throughout the region is the Collared Dove.

disappear at this time of year. On visiting a large fodder field we found over a hundred, far outnumbering the resident Palm Dove population. Many of these birds lacked the neck patch, indicating they were young ones. The next summer they were there again, and again we spotted lots of juveniles. We were intrigued.

Our answer lay about 60 kilometres down the road. Another bird-watcher had found upwards of 50 birds breeding in an old-established palm grove. It would appear that Turtle Doves come to these cultivated areas to breed during the hot summer months. Usually the nest is just below the canopy of palm fronds, with the platform placed on an old cut-back frond. One nest was only a few metres off the sand in a young palm. It was in the shade and contained the usual two white eggs. As this was in early July the chicks were going to make a very hot entrance into this world before flying off to join their relatives at the fodder field kindergarten — hopefully, to return next summer.

Finally, we have the Collared Dove which has a nice black and white collar to aid identification. Otherwise it's a fairly plain pale brown bird, unlike the previous species. We see these along the coasts and they appear to nest in the mangroves. This bird is a sizeable 32 centimetres and you could not be blamed for calling it a pigeon.

The Collared Dove is infamous for its colonisation of western Europe and is beginning to expand within the UAE, where it used to be fairly uncommon. The very typical dove-like 'coo-oo-oo' call is worth remembering while differentiating the 'laughing' Palm Dove from the 'purring' Turtle Dove.

All doves are seed-eaters and not always popular with the farming community. They are also considered to taste rather nice. However, their popularity is not restricted to humans and they are sometimes referred to as 'falcon fodder', a bird family they unwillingly help to sustain.

Top of the falcon's menu is the Grey Francolin, a partridge indigenous to this region. Usually you hear them before you see them — standing in a wood you may hear a loud ringing repetitive call, almost like an exceptionally loud telephone pager. That's our bird. Typical of partridges, they are good runners and difficult to spot amongst the undergrowth. They are usually sighted as they explode into flight from beneath your feet, giving you such a start that it's only after you recover that you begin trying to figure out what it was, and by then it's usually too late.

The Grey Francolin is a brown bird of around 30 centimetres in size. This doesn't sound a very interesting description but if you are lucky and get close to one — even luckier if you have your camera with you — the brown comes alive. The back is resolved into panels and bars of cream, chestnut and rich dark browns. The patterns that are revealed are beautiful but it doesn't stop there; it has a yellowish throat, the belly is barred and there's a bar over the eyes. The explosion of whirring wings which announces the bird's presence, and the start it gives you, are usually the only contacts with the bird.

Having recovered from an exploding Grey Francolin, if you continue your leisurely stroll through a plantation, with Palm Doves winging away on squeaking wings overhead, don't forget to look at the base of the trees. There you may find one of our favourite birds of the region, the Rufous Bush Chat, a Middle East thrush and a close relative of the Nightingale, a migrant here.

These lovely birds have long tails which they cannot leave alone. They seem to be overly conscious of them and are forever fanning and flicking them but mainly trying to lift them over their heads. With most birds the profile from the head,

A Grey Francolin proving to be anything but 'grey'.

down the back to the tail runs straight, some being more upright, others more horizontal in their posture. Not the Bush Chat, the line in a typical stance runs down the back and up the tail.

It has a dull brown back, a prominent pale stripe above the eyes and a large rufous tail, the end of which is tipped black and white. So if you're looking at a thrush-like bird and the most prominent feature you recall is the tail, you've probably been looking at a Rufous Bush Chat. Although we've never found a nest, we are sure they breed here.

All the previous birds and many more besides tend to reside in the large regimented ghaf or acacia plantations which can be pretty frustrating bird-watching sites. A good strategy is needed to get the most out of these trees planted in their strict geometric patterns. We find walking in parallel, two or three avenues apart, yields the best results — or startles the maximum number of birds. What you disturb your partner sees, and vice versa. Working alone in this type of plantation often results in a disappointing search, with the birds usually calling from just beyond the next row of trees.

Often by the roadside or in more arid areas in dried-out water courses there are patches of flowering shrubs known as 'Calotropis' or Sodom's Apple. The large thick-skinned waxy dull green leaves are crowned with pretty pink and white flower clusters. Buzzing around the flower heads you may see a tiny bird hovering, reminiscent of

A Rufous Bush Chat in characteristic surroundings and pose, with its distinctively cocked tail.

a large insect. Like an insect the bird moves from flower to flower in rapid jerky movements on invisible wings, making regular metallic 'zip-zip' calls as it progresses. Looking through binoculars you notice that the bird shines and its bill is relatively long and decurved. This is a Purple Sunbird. Sunbirds are the old-world equivalent of the Hummingbirds of the new world. Calotropis is popular with Sunbirds but we've rarely seen any other birds feeding on them, which is a bit unusual.

From the bill and the frequent hovering it is apparent that they live on the nectar of flowers. And the plumage in breeding males reflects the sun and shines like a jewel. At only 10 centimetres in length the Purple Sunbird is the smallest bird around.

The glistening males contrast with the greenery and flowers in which they live alongside the drab females which are dull brown with creamy underparts, but the size and the bill are still distinctive. Sunbirds build unusual hanging nests. The ball-like base has a side entrance through which the bill can be seen protruding during incubation of the eggs.

Outside the breeding season the males lose their gloss and resemble the females but retain various degrees of purple, often as a stripe running from the throat to the belly. But in the breeding season they glisten and shine and are worthy of the name 'Sunbirds'.

In the older and better-established plantations the perimeters are sheltered by long sedge-like hedges, or fruit tree groves where you may come across another group of small birds. You will not see one by itself as these are very friendly birds. Unlike the sunbird these have a short, heavy, conical, light-coloured, seed-eating bill. This being their most prominent feature, they are aptly named Indian Silverbills.

They have conspicuous black eyes, a brown back, pale undersides and a large silver bill together with a black, pointed tail and white rump. They twitter away and fly around in small flocks full of togetherness. One day we watched a feeding party

Without doubt, the most recognisable of the region's birds is the Hoopoe or 'bud-bud'.

Common along the roadsides, a Crested Lark.

A family group of small Indian Silverbills.

moving one by one from one tree to the next. Each gave a little twitter as it flew across the gap. Then they all flew off together in a swarm, but for some reason one was left behind. The twitter, usually ever so light, grew more mournful with each note; the bird was obviously unhappy being separated from its family. It then flew off in their direction still sounding in a bit of a panic. The social bonds in this family of small birds seem to be very special.

Whether originally indigenous or imported, the Silverbills are making a success of colonising these new cultivations and are a pleasant addition to any plantation.

The following birds can only be seen during the spring or autumn migrations and seem to prefer the quieter cultivated areas to the busier parks and gardens. For this reason we've arbitrarily placed them in this chapter.

When thinking of colourful birds one of the most spectacular is the European Roller, even more so than the related and resident Indian Roller. Its bright, shining, turquoise-blue plumage has to be seen to be appreciated. The back is chestnut, and there's purple and black in the wings and tail. Furthermore, European Rollers do not skulk in the depths of bushes but sit on prominent dead trees or fence posts — they can be very accommodating and a delight to watch. About the size of a crow, they have a distinctive course 'kak-kak - kakka-kaw' call, to attract your attention should you fail to notice the plumage.

These are heavy-billed insect-eaters with a name that depicts their aerobatic flight. Compared with all the little brown birds around, this superbly coloured bright blue bird sitting on a perch is hard to mistake. If you're not at the coast or in Hatta and it's the migration season, then you may safely assume that's a European Roller, without fear of contradiction.

Should you see a black and white striped bird flying like an enormous butterfly, then you may safely say, "That's a Hoopoe". This must be among the most famous of birds, and easy to identify, especially when it sticks its large crown feathers up in the air. Hoopoes are well-represented in Arabian folklore and have a variety of names such as 'hud-hud', which is similar to the bird's call, and locally 'abu al aal' which refers to its crest.

Hoopoes are usually found in groups, probing the ground for grubs, and with a long decurved bill they are well-equipped to find them. They then fly off some distance to the next grub site. The broad, shining, finger-like wings of black and white bring a shock of contrasting colours as they flutter off. They alight and immediately stick up their crests but by the time you focus your camera, they've put them down again. They repeat the performance many times and repeatedly you fail to get a photograph of that raised crest that everyone is so familiar with.

These colourful birds make ideal photographic models, particularly as they do not hide in the

A male Stonechat on a modern perch.

A male Whinchat resting on a goat-trimmed bush.

depths of bushes. Many are frequently seen perched along fences bordering cultivations and can be easily spotted. You may have a dramatic effect on other road users as you screech to a halt along a straight road having almost missed a roller or a chat sitting contentedly on a fence awaiting a passing insect. Provided the subject has not flown off due to the screeching tyres, we then nonchalantly attempt to sidle up to it. For photography, the closer the better — but not at the expense of losing the bird. Judging how close to approach the subject has led to many an argument — and it's always the driver's fault! If we are successful, we're too busy photographing for discussion, but an unsuccessful attempt has been debated for days.

Often found under these circumstances, and the subject of many arguments, are the beautifully coloured Stonechats and Whinchats, which can easily be confused with each other. Both are small, 13-centimetre members of the thrush family. The male Stonechat is easily recognised, with its black head, red breast and white sides to the neck. Problems only arise in trying to distinguish between female Stonechats and Whinchats. The females with their drab colouring always prove to be the most difficult to identify. However, the Whinchat has a bright white obvious supercilium or eyebrows and white tail patches. The female Stonechat has 'eyebrows' also, but they're never that obvious. Both these birds perch in a prominent place and often bob and flick their tails — a good recognition feature. From this perch they launch themselves on to insects, spied on the ground. They are called chats because of their call, a harsh 'chat-chat' which sounds like two stones being struck together.

Leave the plantations, fences and borders behind and have a look for some scrub — small bushes or tufts of grass sparsely spread over the waste land — whether natural or the result of run-off water from nearby gardens. It's often possible to drive amongst the scrub. There's a good chance of seeing wheatears in these areas — there's also the risk of getting stuck in the sand.

This large and varied family of birds is well-represented in the Middle East. Along with large families of birds come identification problems — beyond the scope of this book and it must be said, often even beyond that of the dedicated bird-watchers — especially between the females and non-breeding males, so we'll concentrate on the more colourful and picturesque males. We've already looked at some wheatears so we assume you are familiar with the family by now.

Typical of these scrub areas are the Pied and Desert Wheatears. Pied males, as their name implies, are black and white. They have white crowns, bellies and sides to their tails. The rest is black and often they have rufous tinges on the breast. When looking at similar wheatears we tend to concentrate on the tail — not an easy job as it's best seen in flight or when alighting. But if you do see it, the Pied Wheatears do not have a standard wheatear 'T' but only a very narrow bar to the end of the tail, with thicker edges.

The Desert Wheatear can also best be identified by its tail. Its tail is all black, but it still has a white rump. Confusing? Yes, and it gets worse.

The male Desert Wheatear is a very attractive bird with a black face, bib and wings, contrasting with the sandy-coloured upper parts — from which it may get its name — a white rump and of course that black tail.

Before leaving wheatears, the Isabelline Wheatear needs a mention. In this species the male and female are identical and as the name implies, they are brown birds. Consequently, quite a number are reported. It is renowned for its upright stance and stout body, but for the discerning bird-watcher, once again the identity lies in the tail. In this case a broad bar with only a small 'T' section.

So while observing a wheatear, when all else fails concentrate on the tail — most species can be differentiated if the tail is seen clearly. Practice is needed to achieve this feat as at rest the tail, or rather the distinctive part of it, is covered by the

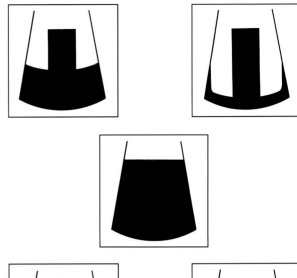

Wheatears' tails are important identification features.
Top left: Northern; top right: Pied; centre: Desert; bottom left: Isabelline; bottom right: Hooded.

wings. If you persevere you will be rewarded; you'll also be well on your way to becoming a bird-watcher and will no longer be conscious of the funny looks you get from non-birders while pursuing a wheatear's tail.

Still in the migration season, you may see a Corn

A male Pied Wheatear usually found along the edges of cultivated areas.

The tail of this Isabelline Wheatear is the best way of confirming the bird's identity.

This distinctive male Desert Wheatear also sports a unique tail pattern.

Bunting or an Ortolan Bunting. The Corn Bunting is usually found perched in trees and the Ortolan on the ground. The ones we photographed changed places, giving added meaning to the word 'usually' ... a word frequently used in bird field guides.

Buntings are a group of sparrow-sized birds in which the males are normally brightly coloured and the females are again often difficult to differentiate. The bill is short and used for cracking seeds. Our photograph shows a beautiful male Ortolan, one of a pair which were resting following migration. They seemed very tired, their eyes closing occasionally, and this allowed our close approach. Neither of the birds flew off and as we retired after photographing them, no doubt they fell into a well-deserved sleep.

The most striking feature on the Ortolan is the large moustacial stripe which resembles a sergeant major's moustache. You also notice the subtle green and yellow washes of the face, and the chestnut belly. Typical of buntings the back has boldy marked patterns of different shades of brown. The female does not show these colours but the moustache can usually be seen, though not as distinctly as on the male — as befits a female's moustache.

By way of contrast, the large Corn Bunting's plumage is a mixture of streaked browns, being lighter on the underparts. Your attention is always brought back to the head of this bird with its very marked face and enormous bill. Whereas normally birds have round heads to which a bill has been stuck on, the Corn Bunting's bill seems to be an extension of the forehead.

These birds are invariably seen in groups and have a sweet 'prit-prit-prit' call which they issue while changing position from bush to bush.

The worst bird-watching identification problems inevitably involve brown birds. In these cases it's important to look at the shape of the bird, observe its behaviour and to listen to its call, if it does call. To illustrate this, compare the bulky Corn Bunting with its upright posture and enormous bill to a much smaller brown bird, half of which is tail, found in bushes where it never stops twitching. It is restless and as it flies, it seems to drag its tail along like a streamer behind it. The call is a continuous buzzing noise which it delivers from the top of a bush. It is named the Graceful Warbler, which obviously does not refer to its flight. This bird breeds here and is spreading out to occupy many cultivated areas. Those straggly bushes, Salvadora persica, found between the acacia avenues, are a favourite site of the Graceful Warbler.

A colourful migrant European Roller.

An Ortolan Bunting, resting.

The massive-billed Corn Bunting seen searching for grain in a fodder field.

Nesting Olivaceous Warblers can be found in Abu Dhabi's Bateen Wood.

Blue-cheeked Bee-eaters are usually heard well before they are seen.

Staying on the brown bird theme, the Crested Lark solves most identification problems by having a large head crest. These birds were rarely found as far east as Abu Dhabi until recently, but can now be found virtually throughout the Emirates.

Also, there's something about the way a lark flies that differentiates it from, say a pipit. Larks seem to open and close their broad wings almost as you open and extend your fingers from a closed fist. Most other birds wave their wings up and down. Larks fly differently but are still brown.

One more bird deserves mention: the Olivaceous Warbler which used to cause us many identification problems. This is a real little brown job with no obvious features to rely on. First it's a warbler, full of restless energy. Many a frustrated bird-watcher is convinced this is to make them harder to identify in the trees. For a warbler, it is heavy-billed and stocky and fortunately it constantly flicks its tail in a very characteristic shallow manner. Then it calls, lots of gibberish with harsh notes amongst the general warbling.

We've found several nests of the Olivaceous Warbler in Bateen Woods right in the centre of Abu Dhabi. Little cup-shaped affairs into which the bird hardly seems to fit, head protruding out on one side and tail out the other.

A few weeks later the wood is filled with families of youngsters clinging to branches and clamouring to be fed by the overworked adults.

After a stroll through a plantation, a drive through scrub and a period of fence spotting, it's pleasant to return to the fodder fields. In these enormous tracts of green grass it's difficult to believe that you are in the middle of an arid desert. On our summer visits attention focussed on the breeding Turtle Doves; but return in the winter and the scene changes.

In these fields the grass is cut monthly, so there's always closely cropped grass, with pipits and wagtails scratching about, and mature long grass where chats and bee-eaters rest on the sprinklers, which make good perches for our models. Similar in size, shape and actions to the more colourful European Bee-eaters, the Blue-cheeked Bee-eaters are a lovely green colour. They have a dark eyestripe, beneath which lies the blue cheek. More noticeable is the yellow chin, chestnut throat and the red-orange underwings which suddenly become visible as the bird takes flight to sing its less musical 'prrt-prrt' call.

There is so much potential food about that birds of prey abound. The most likely species to be spotted is the Kestrel. A small falcon, it is readily identified as it is the only falcon which hovers high over the fields. Good views of the Kestrel show the males to have a grey head and tail with a black terminal bar. Both sexes have beautiful chestnut backs, spotted in black.

Birds of prey are always exciting to watch. With the falcons it's their flying skills — little can compare with a peregrine in a swoop, as it crashes into a pigeon amidst an explosion of feathers. With Kestrels you marvel at how they hover, keeping their heads absolutely stationary while searching for their prey before dropping out of the sky onto an unsuspecting victim.

We've also seen large Long-legged Buzzards either perched or soaring, and even powerful eagles and dashing hawks can be found. But these large fields are an ideal habitat for harriers. These long-tailed hunters with long-fingered wings search the fields for food by quartering the area, just above the ground, on raised wings. Commonest of this family is the Pallid Harrier but all four harrier species have been seen. The male Pallid is light grey with diamond-shaped black feather patches at the edges of the wings. The females are, as usual, a little more difficult to identify.

Collectively, the female Pallid, Hen and Montagu's Harriers are known as ring tails — due to their banded tails. They also have bright white rumps. The species are difficult to differentiate but in flight the Pallid and Montagu's Harriers are more airy or tern-like. If you can get close enough, it is better to look at the face patterns — the Pallid is well marked and has a ring almost encircling the neck whereas on Montagu's only the eyes are highlighted.

All these fields, woods and other cultivations provide food and shelter in an otherwise inhospitable area and as they continue to grow so do our bird-watching opportunities.

A passage migrant that hunts in fodder fields is the Pallid Harrier.

A rare Montagu's Harrier resting after quartering the fields in search of a Pipit or Wagtail.

A small falcon, this beautiful male Kestrel poses atop a sprinkler.

Large White Storks, once uncommon, are beginning to increase in number as are the fodder fields in which they are found.

Eagle Owl chicks, aged about one month, at their
nest site (inset) on a crag in the desert.

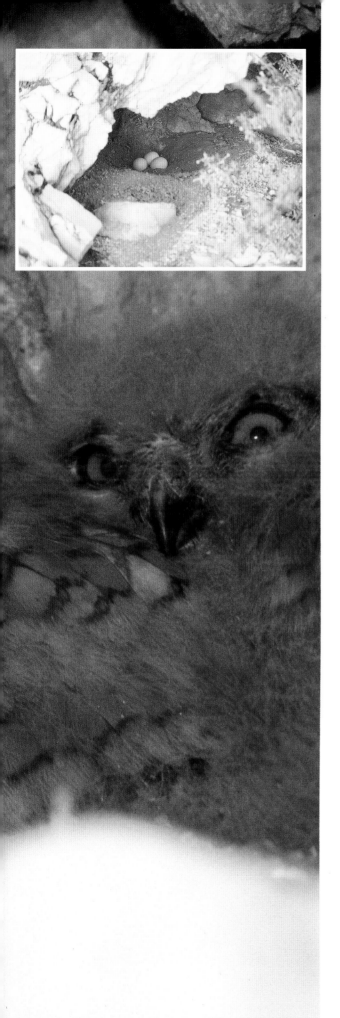

THE DESERT
hostile yet habitable

A very common English saying in this part of the world is, "It's tough in the Gulf", probably coined years ago during the hot, humid summers before the advent of air conditioners. The sequel to this must be, "It's hell in the desert". A great many people now reside in desert areas, particularly in oil camps which these days provide luxurious accommodation and cuisine. But in the summer when your car gets stuck or you're forced to labour outdoors you realise that it can still be hell in the desert. And yet, birds are not only found here but breed and rear offspring in this hostile environment. Although some mention is made of the migrants which seasonally pass back and forth through the deserts, most of this chapter is dedicated to the resident desert birds and their survival.

First the migrants. Outside the really hot summer months, the deserts of the Emirates, which border on the Empty Quarter, are relatively pleasant areas. There is adequate vegetation to support sizeable camel herds and of course an amazing variety and number of birds.

An oilfield camp, with its trees, lawns and ample water supply makes an ideal area to watch the migrants and winter visitors. They are almost magnetically attracted to these man-made oases. Having discovered the presence of birds, as a bird-watcher you become thoroughly amazed at the often uncharacteristic species which can be seen. Almost all the waders and herons have been seen, even sea gulls and ducks. All are on migration, suggesting that migration occurs over a very broad area and not just on established routes.

Most of the birds of prey can be seen and all the passerines or perching birds. Several of the new species found in the UAE have originated from our desert observation points. These include the Namaqua Dove, an Eye-browed Thrush and most recently a Grey-headed Kingfisher. Most of the birds are true migrants and visit for two to five days, whereupon having replenished their reserves, they leave to continue their journey. The true migration picture may never be known as most migration occurs at night. So on discovering a single Lapwing or Starling in the camp you can only presume that the remainder of the flock flew on past.

Other birds are termed winter visitors and stay from autumn through to spring. During this period large flocks of White Wagtails are found; Water Pipits, Chiffchaffs and Isabelline Shrikes are also good examples of these visitors.

A few species of birds have actually chosen to live in the desert and exploit the often meagre food reserves to be found here. One can only wonder why creatures with the mobility of birds would choose to live in such an adverse environment.

One of this select band is the Eagle Owl. Throughout the world owls are considered to be harbingers of bad luck. That may be so but to bird-watchers they are a very special group of birds. They are unique, with their large forward facing eyes, accentuated by the facial discs and their habit of appearing to be able to rotate their heads through 360 degrees.

Eagle Owls are large birds, of about 50 centimetres, with large ear tufts, sharp beaks and very powerful talons. Like most desert species they blend with their surroundings; being sandy in colour they are difficult to find, even though they are so large. Identification is fairly straightforward as a sandy coloured owl of such large proportions can be little else in the desert.

Observation is complicated, as like most owls, they are nocturnal hunters and are usually only seen in the late evening, having spent the day in some crevice out of the sun. They live on lizards and rodents and sit on a prominent perch listening for the sounds of their prey. They then glide in silent flight to grab the unsuspecting victims with their talons. Their excellent hearing and night vision is the reason behind their success.

All birds have a unique Latin name, and often several English names, the latter reflecting either a geographic location, the original discoverer, or a prominent feature. The Latin names rarely mean a great deal to the average birder. However, the Eagle Owl is known as Bubo bubo which exactly depicts the birds low barking call. It was hearing this call while scrambling over a desert crag that brought our attention to the presence of an Eagle Owl during February. Then a little later a second owl was seen, this time much closer. A search of the area brought us to a nest containing three large white eggs. As we were to find on repeated visits to the area, one

A wide-eyed Stone Curlew demonstrating the effectiveness of its desert camouflage.

A Hoopoe Lark, which is well adapted to running through the desert sands and probing for insects.

of the birds stood on guard duty and called a warning to its mate in the nest, as we, the intruders, approached.

There was no real nest, only a scrape in the sand in a crevice on the crag face. We visited the site a month later to find three down-covered chicks who hissed and clacked their beaks as we approached. On the third and final visit the nest was empty and we eventually found the chicks under a tree higher up the crag. They now began to look like Eagle Owls, even the ear tufts were beginning to form and they were almost full grown. The hissing and clacking sounded more menacing on this visit.

Eagle Owls have been known to inhabit this crag for some years now. According to the literature, these owls marry for life and divorce has not been recorded, so presumably we shall be able to find them in future years. The youngsters move off to find their own mate and crag, and if the above is true, live happily ever after!

Probably the commonest desert resident is the Hoopoe Lark, so called because of the black and white striped Hoopoe-like wing pattern seen in flight. However, those of this region have less barring than the standard model and sometimes show no black, except at the wing tips. These birds are not particularly shy and are frequently seen along desert tracks. They have a tendency to run rather than fly. While running, their bodies are held in an upright stance, and they then stop only to run off again just as you manage to focus the camera. At 18 centimetres they represent a large lark and resemble a pipit in behaviour, rather than a typical lark.

Using their long decurved bills they dig for insects in the sand beneath the sparse vegetation of their chosen habitat. The birds have a lovely flute-like call, that seems to fit the desert terrain in which they are found. One observer described the call exactly as the first three notes of 'God save the Queen', whistled slightly off key. Much whistling

Brown-necked Ravens are superb masters of the air.

accompanies the courtship activities. One bird, presumably the male, shoots up to 20 metres in the air and then glides back to earth, whistling continuously.

We found two nests this year, both of which were built in the top of a small bush, some 40-50 centimetres above the sand. The nest is a woven cup of twigs lined with finer material. Surprisingly, the nests sit on top of the bush in the full glare of the sun, and the birds don't even attempt to make use of the available shade, although, in the height of summer the birds often resort to resting in shaded areas during the hot midday period. On approaching the nest, the birds would run off a little way, and then like plovers pretend to be hurt in order to distract you from the nest site. During this activity the bird often approaches within two metres of the intruder.

At both these nest sites young chicks were found in the nest. Three in one nest and six in the other. Unfortunately neither brood survived. In one case the empty nest site was surrounded by the tracks of Brown-necked Ravens, a desert scavenger and our next desert breeder.

These are the crows of the desert and are around 50 centimetres in size. Like most crows or more particularly ravens they are marvellous fliers. They can be seen in large numbers, outside the breeding season, soaring effortlessly in the thermals — a wonderful sight. It is their flight that is captivating, particularly with over a hundred wheeling around. The other side of their nature, scavenging for food, is not so pleasant.

Identification is straightforward as these are the only black crow-like birds to be found in these desert regions. The related House Crow, a common sight along the coasts, is never seen in the desert — at least not so far. These Brown-necked Ravens have brown necks at certain times of the year when seen at close range and provided the light is correct; not a good identification feature!

They build large nests and typically can be found on ledges of crags. However, being one of the most adaptable of the bird families, they use wellhead markers, electrical poles, lamp stands and disused buildings. In all cases the nests are inaccessible. Unfortunately, where natural twigs are in short supply they use available scrap, particularly discarded copper cable which may often have shocking effects at some of the chosen nest sites.

They are scavengers and opportunist feeders. At one of our desert outposts the grain put out for the sheep is also feeding about a hundred ravens. When you arrive at the sheep enclosure there is an explosion of disturbed black birds, almost like bats leaving the belfry as soon as darkness arrives. However, leaving aside their questionable character, watching their often aerobatic and soaring flight can become an absorbing desert pastime.

Another desert resident is a relative rarity and has the alliterative name of the Cream-coloured Courser. Most bird identification guides and handbooks arrange bird families in a strictly systematic order beginning with ancient birds such as ostriches, divers and grebes and finishing with such modern bird families as finches and buntings. These place bird families of a similar evolutionary background together. However, the Cream-coloured Courser along with the Stone Curlew is found amidst a variety of water birds.

This Courser is another bird that prefers to run rather than fly and is a superb runner at that, with long legs ideally suited for the job. Typical of desert species the bird is a sandy colour and also has very distinctively contrasting black primaries and underwings. When seen close-up, in good light, the black eyestripe, white supercilium and blue-grey rear crown enhance its apparently drab appearance. The bird stands very upright and is around 23 centimetres in size. Living in the desert and desert fringes, it eats lizards and insects for which its running speed and long decurved bill are well developed. The nest is apparently an unlined depression in which two eggs are laid. While we have not yet found a nest we did see a single juvenile with parents on Dalma island — not quite true desert terrain.

A winter visitor and close ally of the Cream-coloured Courser is the secretive Stone Curlew. Resembling a small Houbara, it is known by the Bedu as 'karawan'. It is very difficult to locate when crouched during the day because of its sandy plumage and dark streaking. It is usually only found if accidentally disturbed, whereupon it flies off on black and white pointed wings, only to disappear again unless closely watched.

These birds eat insects which they catch in the evenings and at night. Their large, staring, yellow eyes and long sturdy legs are adaptations, specially designed to make them successful in a desert terrain.

Another desert-breeding bird is the Black-crowned Finch Lark, or BCFL for short. And short they are, in contrast to the birds just discussed, being only 10-12 centimetres in length. They are different from other birds in many ways which are highlighted as follows.

A Cream-coloured Courser, found on Dalma Island.

The male and female have very different plumages. The female is a typical desert bird with a sandy plumage and black underwings, whereas the male has a bold black and white pattern on the head and undersides making it a striking bird to observe. Identification of the female is made by size, black underwing and conical bill, but best confirmed when accompanied by the black and white male, which is usually the case. These birds are gregarious and often seen in flocks of up to a hundred. It is uncommon to see a lone BCFL. Like most social birds, their movements seem to be under a central controller, as they leap-frog from the back of a feeding group to the front, thus moving the group forward. Much calling accompanies these moves. Then in unison the group flies off to a new feeding location.

Another difference is that they are primarily seed-eaters. This is not difficult to believe when you notice the heavy conical bill as compared to the long, often decurved, bill of the insect-eaters.

The birds also nest colonially, in sandy depressions which are lined with hairs or dry grass, in the shadow of a tussock or bush.

The Great Grey Shrike lives and breeds on the fringes of the desert or in small, isolated copses. Small numbers of these birds breed in this region while many more pass through on migration. Typical of shrikes, the Great Greys live on insects which they pounce upon from their prominent perches.

Identification problems can occur between the Great and Lesser Grey Shrikes which are similarly plumaged. To avoid confusion it is safest to look at the extent of exposed wing feathers or primaries. They are quite short in the Great Grey and noticeably longer in the Lesser Grey Shrike. The longer bill, the smaller mask, the less white on the wing, and the overall longer, slimmer appearance, all suggest a Great Grey Shrike, but if possible try and check the wing. Once Great and Lesser Greys are sorted out, look out for the pale-billed or Iranian sub-species of Great Grey Shrike with the Latin name Lanius excubitor pallidirostris. These pass through the region on migration.

The resident birds build nests in trees or bushes, in the form of an untidy lined cup into which three to six eggs are laid. Although we've yet to find a nest, we have seen juveniles around in their much browner plumage.

Before leaving the desert to journey into the mountains, a mention needs to be made of the sandgrouse. These pigeon-like birds have specially modified breast and belly feathers that allow them to carry water over large distances to the nest site. They visit their favourite watering holes usually in the morning or late evening to 'top up' — a real adaptation to desert living.

Near the bottom of Wadi Bih one such watering hole exists. One evening, parked near the pond, we sat and watched until the sun went down. Then in the dark the air became filled with what can best be described as electronic generated noises as parties of Lichtenstein's Sandgrouse flew in, to top up. They were landing all around us, often flying right over our heads. In all we guestimated about 250 — but we were only at one end of the pool. Sitting in the dark amongst all this activity, especially having tried to find these birds all day, was an experience one would wish to repeat, and a fitting way to leave the 'sterile' desert.

A male Black-crowned Finch Lark or BCFL.

A dark-legged Water Pipit, a winter visitor.

Great Grey Shrikes are found perched on scrub on the fringes of the desert, where they dive upon passing prey.

A soaring Egyptian Vulture atop Jebel Hafit where, on the right day, over one hundred can be seen.

MOUNTAINS AND WADIS
rising thermals and running streams

High barren peaks and deeply shaded valleys; soaring vultures and hovering Sunbirds; this is an area of extremes and contrasts, which are reflected in the terrain and in the birds.

One of the most satisfying sights when bird-watching must be that of a vulture effortlessly soaring over a mountain range. With only minute adjustments to the large finger-like feathers at the tip of the wings, these birds control their height and direction. They rarely seem to resort to energy-intensive flapping of their massive wings, but hang in the air defying gravity and drift along. Yet, they achieve great heights, and the distance covered in their search for food is extensive. Watching from the ground, you see them disappearing all too rapidly into the distance, leaving only the empty sky.

Rarely seen in the early morning, the birds often appear around midday when the thermals are well developed. By far the commonest species to be seen in the region are Egyptian and Griffon Vultures. With their enormous broad wings and relatively small heads they are usually readily identified but they could be confused with eagles. The black and white plumage and the wedge-shaped tail of the adult Egyptian Vulture make it the easiest to identify. Often large groups of these can be seen around Jebel Hafit.

It was a visit to Jebel Hafit to photograph these birds that proved to be one of our best bird-watching days even though we didn't see, let alone photograph, an Egyptian Vulture. And on a subsequent visit when we provided a feast of lamb carcasses we still weren't successful. They just sat far away and waited until we left before eating.

Outside a small guardhouse near the top of the mountain, the bored guard had made a very small pond which he regularly filled with water. In the height of summer, water is rare on the mountain top and this became a collection point for birds, and what birds! We were first attracted to the pool by relatively large numbers of Desert Lark. In mountainous areas they seem to fill the gap left by the absence of House Sparrows. Up to 10 birds at a time were alighting at the pond, taking a drink and flying off in search of food or shade.

The Desert Lark is a bird of the mountains as opposed to the deserts and is a typical LBJ (little brown job). Identification is basically made from the structure of the bird rather than any plumage features. Several sub-species of the Desert Lark exist and the overall colour of the plumage changes depending on the bird's specific habitat, varying from sandy brown to dark grey. They occur in small flocks and continually call to each other with a melodious yet mournful series of notes.

Desert Larks appear in a variety of plumages designed to suit their surroundings.

Meanwhile back at the pool, a Hume's Wheatear arrived. These beautiful black and white wheatears are often found in the mountains, and rarely elsewhere. The bird drank and flew off and another arrived. Although black and white and clearly a wheatear it was not a Hume's but a Hooded Wheatear. This splendidly plumaged adult male was one of only a handful to be seen in the Emirates. And then a brown wheatear appeared, another Hooded record and this time a female. These birds are relatively large with elongated bills and heads, not rounded as in Hume's Wheatear, for example. The tail pattern is also unique consisting of a central bar and white sides, but no 'T' at the tip of the tail so typical of wheatears. There is relatively little known about these birds, which are found in desolate, barren areas, where they live on a diet of insects. Like Hume's, they are capable of surviving the intense heat.

Since our visit to the pool took place during May and again in June, these birds were not on migration,

and are thought to be breeding in the area. On a later visit, in addition to these birds, two more individuals arrived, and finally a young male Hooded appeared. In addition to finding rare birds at the pool, today you can also find an even rarer species in this area — bird-watchers.

Most of the activity at the pool took place during the morning but in the heat of the early afternoon the Hooded Wheatears were still visiting, frequently hovering above the pool's surface, before drinking from it. The birds never arrived together, always singly. Between visits of Hooded Wheatears, occasionally a House Bunting arrived, a beautifully marked male.

House Buntings are about 14 centimetres in size and have notched bunting tails and short, stout bills for opening seeds. The heads are striped black and white or buff and they have chestnut wings. The females, typical of this group, are less colourful and can be difficult to separate from other female buntings. House Buntings are usually only found in these areas of mountains and wadis, and generally occur in groups.

It was hot now, with the sun reflecting off the barren rocks, and the excitement of the Hooded Wheatears was melting away. Thoughts of returning to an air-conditioned house were getting stronger — but these soon disappeared. Almost unnoticed a pair of small birds arrived along with one of the Hooded Wheatears. They were small, only 12 centimetres, with a large bright red conical bill, subtle pink and lilac colouring in the grey-brown body and black conspicuous eyes. They were Trumpeter Finches and a rare record for the UAE. We didn't feel hot now as we photographed the birds drinking at the pool.

These finches are so named because their call is said to resemble a child's trumpet and can be heard over long distances. We'd seen flocks of these birds earlier in the year across the border in Oman. At neither time did we hear the famous trumpet call. Something to look forward to in future encounters.

On our next visit to the pool both the Hooded Wheatears and a single Trumpeter Finch were seen, but that was not the day's highlight. We saw a Sand Partridge, a small partridge which inhabits mountainous areas. It had come to the pool for a drink and brought its family. First one, then another and yet another running chick appeared in sight until a total of 19 were running after the adult. What a sight! They crossed the road, then recrossed it, with many of the young struggling to ascend the high concrete barriers on either side. There was

An uncommon male Hooded Wheatear.

A very distinctive House Bunting of the mountains.

much flapping of wings and small sortie flights and continuous calling to each other. They approached the pool, but unhappy at our presence, ran off down the mountainside and out of sight.

Other members of this family are the Chukar and the See-see Partridge, both of which are named after their very distinctive calls — the Chukar having a harsh 'chuck-chuck-chuck chukaar' and the See-see having a more muted 'see-see-see' whistle. Many of these birds have been introduced to the region.

We had seen the odd Chukar before, then one day we bumped our way up Wadi Bih. Typical of our more successful journeys we'd missed our original objective, but decided to see what was beyond the next bend. After negotiating many bends we decided to take a break and let our internal organs settle back into their normal positions. The shade provided by a group of trees seemed a likely spot to rest.

Here, our attention was drawn to a pair of White-cheeked Bulbuls, which were a long way from their typical city woodland habitats. The subsequent discussion was interrupted by the continuous 'chuk, chuk, chuk' calls. Then we heard the full song as the Chukar announced its presence.

Mountain songsters, Yellow-vented Bulbuls.

A small valley cut into the wadi where we sat, which on inspection showed some very old signs of human habitation. Further up this cut, the calling of Chukars increased and then we saw them swarming over the large rocks. Although occasionally flying very short distances, this group of around 80 birds was running up the mountainside in typical partridge fashion.

Leaving the peaks and descending into the wadis, the scenery and the birds change. When there's water in the wadis many wader species can be found, although rarely in large numbers. Of the sandpipers, both Wood and Green Sandpipers occur.

Other water birds include the Grey Wagtail. This is the largest of the wagtails, being longer tailed than the others, and it has a distinctive grey back and yellow rump. You can also find the Red-wattled Lapwing, a very attractive and distinctively marked plover. The call of this bird, which it utters repeatedly at the least provocation has been exactly translated into English as 'did-he-do-it'. We renamed it the 'Did-he-do-it', a much nicer name than the far more formal Red-wattled Lapwing. These birds breed in the region.

The trees and scrub lining the wadis provide a suitable habitat for the Yellow-vented Bulbul and the Arabian Babbler. We haven't renamed these as

Arabian Babblers displaying the long tail which makes them easy to identify.

they are sufficiently fanciful already. The Yellow-vented Bulbul is the mountain version of the White-cheeked Bulbul so often seen in the lowland parks. Because of its black head and light eye-ring, one of our associates thought it resembled a terrorist in the photograph. With a sweet, tuneful repertoire of songs, it is the most melodious of songbirds up in the mountains.

The Arabian Babbler is usually seen in groups, or a better description would be gangs, of four or five or more. They seem to play a continuous game of chase as they fly from bush to bush, maniacally crashing into the centre, only to emerge from a different location and hurtle into the next bush. They also hop around, tail in the air, playing the babbler version of tag. Crazy birds! Although brown they can be easily identified by their large size, around 28 centimetres, of which about 50 per cent is made up of a long graduated tail.

In Fossil Valley, a wide fertile plain between ridges, you can find the Yellow-throated Sparrow, a rather thin-billed sparrow. Our photograph shows a very untypically bright-yellow-throated individual. Usually the yellow throat is very subdued and is only noticeable on close inspection. Better identification features are the plain back, chestnut wing patch and white wing bars.

Perched on the larger trees or overhead powerlines is the very pretty Little Green Bee-eater. This beautiful green flier bursts into flight in pursuit of insects and exposes a bright orange underwing. They nest colonially in holes burrowed out of sandy bank sides. Confusion is possible with the larger migratory Blue-cheeked Bee-eater, which is rarely seen in the mountains.

When we visit Fossil Valley we usually camp near the sheer sides, leaving the plain to the goats and camels. One morning we noticed a Kestrel, which

A Red-wattled Lapwing.

Grey Wagtail, in a wadi.

Red-tailed Wheatear.

Yellow-throated Sparrow.

A male Blue Rock Thrush which is most often found in mountainous areas.

A Sand Partridge and family, in search of a morning drink atop Jebel Hafit.

had a nest in the cliff, being harrassed by another bird. Surely the wrong way round; Kestrels are usually the attackers! The attacker this time turned out to be a Little Owl which had a nest only 20 metres from the Kestrel's. These Little Owls are diurnal and nest in holes in the cliff. Although they are only 22 centimetres long they are aggressive. When annoyed they bob up and down and try to outstare you with their large yellow eyes.

While sitting in a nice cool wadi, if you look upwards you will inevitably see a Pale Crag Martin on one of its ceaseless patrols along the wadi. These birds are rarely seen to perch or rest, and fly very close to the walls of the wadi in their constant search for insects. Typical of martins and swallows they build a cup-shaped nest of mud, which is 'glued' to a crevice on a cliff face. They are usually seen in pairs, in flight, and are rarely found alone.

Midway between the peaks and wadis live the wheatears and the Blue Rock Thrush. The commonest wheatear is the Hume's, but not all the Hume's are Hume's. A careful inspection could reveal an Eastern Pied Wheatear. This bird resembles a poorly turned-out Hume's, the plumage having a brownish tinge instead of being glossy black. Also, the sharp separation of black and white on the breast of Hume's is diffused on this bird. A closer look does show similarities in structure to the more common Pied Wheatear. We see a few of these birds during the migration season; some overwinter.

In these same areas you can also find the Red-tailed Wheatear. This bird's rather boring plumage is redeemed, fortunately for bird-watchers, by a bright orange rump, vent and tail. It is usually found prominently perched on a bush, from which it hawks passing insects.

Rounding off our tour we find the Blue Rock Thrush and a male in breeding plumage justifying its descriptive title. About 20 centimetres, they resemble thrushes in appearance and can be seen perched on rocks on the hill sides. Unfortunately, the females are brown, not blue, and must first be identified by their shape as being Rock Thrushes. The absence of an orange rump then confirms them to be the Blue species as opposed to being just Rock Thrushes.

Well we hope you enjoyed the tour; we certainly did, and our pictures — all of which have a tale behind them, some of which we can't or don't wish to discuss — leave us with happy memories of birding in this region. If we have enticed anyone to consider joining the growing ranks of bird-watchers, who go where no man has gone before, binoculars in-hand and a field guide in the pocket, then it has been well-worth the effort.

A menacing Little Owl, near its nest site which is a hole in a sheer cliff face.

An Eastern Pied Wheatear.

Commoner Hume's Wheatear.

A rare Trumpeter Finch.

Little Green Bee-eater.

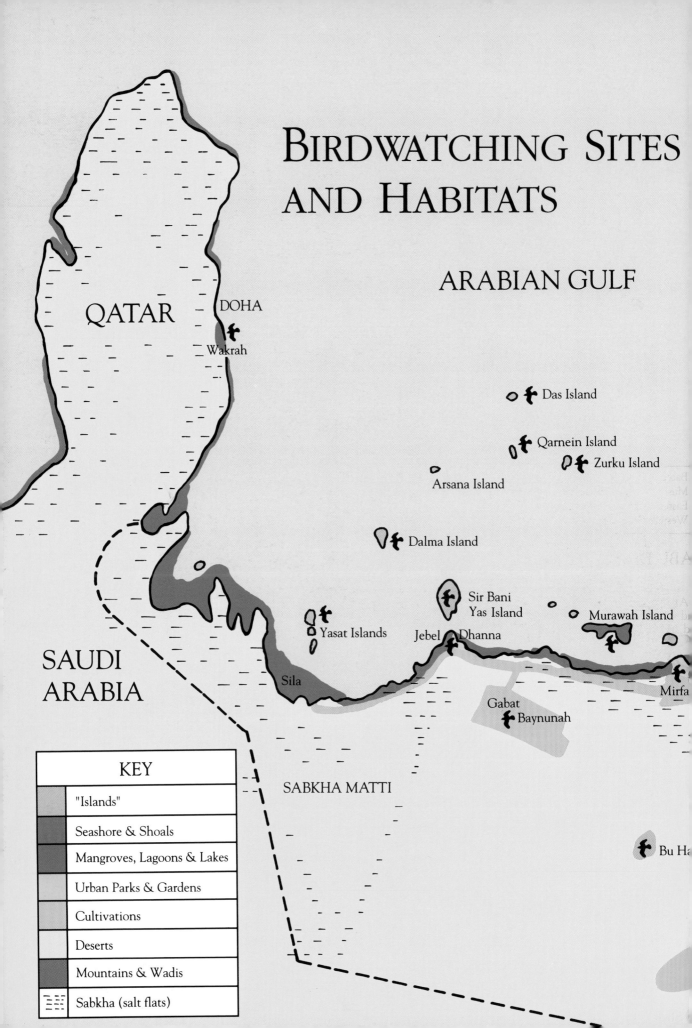

BIRDWATCHING SITES AND HABITATS

ARABIAN GULF

QATAR

DOHA

Wakrah

Das Island

Qarnein Island

Zurku Island

Arsana Island

Dalma Island

Sir Bani Yas Island

Murawah Island

Yasat Islands

Jebel Dhanna

SAUDI ARABIA

Sila

Mirfa

Gabat Baynunah

SABKHA MATTI

Bu Ha

KEY	
	"Islands"
	Seashore & Shoals
	Mangroves, Lagoons & Lakes
	Urban Parks & Gardens
	Cultivations
	Deserts
	Mountains & Wadis
	Sabkha (salt flats)

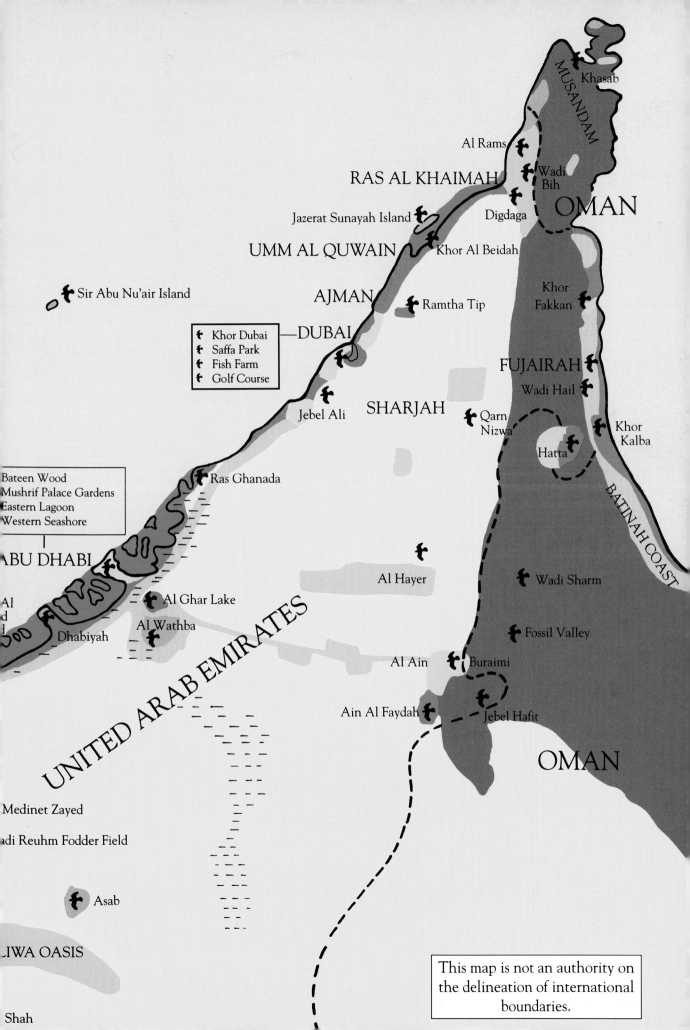

Khasab

MUSANDAM

Al Rams

Wadi Bih

RAS AL KHAIMAH

Digdaga

OMAN

Jazerat Sunayah Island

UMM AL QUWAIN

Khor Al Beidah

Khor Fakkan

AJMAN

Ramtha Tip

Sir Abu Nu'air Island

Khor Dubai
Saffa Park
Fish Farm
Golf Course

DUBAI

FUJAIRAH

Wadi Hail

Qarn Nizwa

Khor Kalba

Jebel Ali

SHARJAH

Hatta

BATINAH COAST

Bateen Wood
Mushrif Palace Gardens
Eastern Lagoon
Western Seashore

Ras Ghanada

ABU DHABI

Al Hayer

Wadi Sharm

Al
d
l

Al Ghar Lake

Dhabiyah

Al Wathba

UNITED ARAB EMIRATES

Fossil Valley

Al Ain

Buraimi

Ain Al Faydah

Jebel Hafit

OMAN

Medinet Zayed

di Reuhm Fodder Field

Asab

IWA OASIS

Shah

This map is not an authority on the delineation of international boundaries.

CHECKLIST

☑ Little Grebe *Tachybaptus ruficollis*, 39, 41

☐ Great Crested Grebe *Podiceps cristatus*

☐ Red-necked Grebe *Podiceps grisegena*

☑ Black-necked Grebe *Podiceps nigricollis*, 39

☐ Jouanin's Petrel *Bulweria fallax*

☐ Flesh-footed Shearwater *Puffinus carneipes*

☐ Wedge-tailed Shearwater *Puffinus pacificus*

☐ Audubon's Shearwater *Puffinus lherminieri*

☐ Wilson's Storm-Petrel *Oceanites oceanicus*

☐ Leach's Storm-Petrel *Oceanodroma leucorhoa*

☑ Red-billed Tropic-bird *Phaethon aethereus*, 19

☐ Red-footed Booby *Sula sula*

☐ Masked Booby *Sula dactylatra*

☐ Brown Booby *Sula leucogaster*

☑ Great Cormorant *Phalacrocorax carbo*, 25

☑ Socotra Cormorant
Phalacrocorax nigrogularis, 24, 25, 28, 29

☐ White Pelican *Pelecanus onocrotalus*

☐ Dalmatian Pelican *Pelecanus crispus*

☐ Bittern *Botaurus stellaris*

☐ Little Bittern *Ixobrychus minutus*

☐ Night Heron *Nycticorax nycticorax*

☑ Little Green Heron *Butorides striatus*, 37

☑ Squacco Heron *Ardeola ralloides*, 37

☐ Indian Pond Heron *Ardeola grayii*

☑ Cattle Egret *Bubulcus ibis*, 58

☑ Western Reef Heron *Egretta gularis*, 35, 36, 37

☑ Little Egret *Egretta garzetta*, 36, 37

☑ Great White Egret *Egretta alba*, 36, 41

☑ Grey Heron *Ardea cinerea*, 36, 41

☐ Purple Heron *Ardea purpurea*

☐ Black Stork *Ciconia nigra*

☑ White Stork *Ciconia ciconia*, 77

☑ Glossy Ibis *Plegadis falcinellus*, 58

☐ Sacred Ibis *Threskiornis aethiopicus*

☑ Spoonbill *Platalea leucorodia*, 36

☑ Greater Flamingo *Phoenicopterus ruber*, 36

☐ Mute Swan *Cygnus olor*

☐ White-fronted Goose *Anser albifrons*

☑ Greylag Goose *Anser anser*, 56

☑ Egyptian Goose *Alopochen aegyptiacus*, 37, 45

☐ Ruddy Shelduck *Tadorna ferruginea*

☐ Shelduck *Tadorna tadorna*

☐ Cotton Teal *Nettapus coromandelianus*

☑ Wigeon *Anas penelope*, 38

☐ Gadwall *Anas strepera*

☑ Teal *Anas crecca*, 38, 43

☑ Mallard *Anas platyrhynchos*, 38, 43

☑ Pintail *Anas acuta*, 38

☑ Garganey *Anas querquedula*, 38

☑ Shoveller *Allas clypeata*, 38

☐ Marbled Teal *Marmaronetta angustirostris*

☐ Red-crested Pochard *Netta rufina*

☑ Pochard *Aythya ferina*, 38, 43

☑ Ferruginous Duck *Aythya nyroca*, 38

☑ Tufted Duck *Aythya fuligula*, 38

☐ Red-breasted Merganser *Mergus serrator*

☐ Honey Buzzard *Pernis apivorus*

☐ Black-shouldered Kite *Elanus caeruleus*

☐ Black Kite *Milvus migrans*

☐ Brahminy Kite *Haliastur indus*

☐ Pallas's Fish Eagle *Haliaeetus leucoryphus*

☑ Egyptian Vulture *Neophron percnopterus*, 86, 87

☑ Griffon Vulture *Gyps fulvus*, 87

☐ Lappet-faced Vulture *Torgos tracheliotus*

☐ Short-toed Eagle *Circaetus gallicus*

☑ Marsh Harrier *Circus aeruginosus*, 56

☑ Hen Harrier *Circus cyaneus*, 74

☑ Pallid Harrier *Circus macrourus*, 74

☑ Montagu's Harrier *Circus pygargus*, 74, 75

☐ Dark Chanting Goshawk *Melierax metabates*

☐ Goshawk *Accipiter gentilis*

☑ Sparrowhawk *Accipiter nisus*, 51

☐ Levant Sparrowhawk *Accipiter brevipes*

☐ Buzzard *Buteo buteo*

☑ Long-legged Buzzard *Buteo rufinus*, 74

☐ Lesser Spotted Eagle *Aquila pomarina*

☐ Spotted Eagle *Aquila clanga*

☐ Steppe Eagle *Aquila nipalensis*

☐ Imperial Eagle *Aquila heliaca*

☐ Golden Eagle *Aquila chrysaetos*

☐ Booted Eagle *Hieraaetus pennatus*

☐ Bonelli's Eagle *Hieraaetus fasciatus*

☑ Osprey *Pandion haliaetus*, 24

☐ Lesser Kestrel *Falco naumanni*

☑ Kestrel *Falco tinnunculus*, 73, 74, 76, 91, 94

☐ Merlin *Falco columbarius*

☑ Hobby *Falco subbuteo*, 14

☑ Sooty Falcon *Falco concolor*, 11, 13, 14, 17

☐ Lanner Falcon *Falco biarmicus*

☐ Saker Falcon *Falco cherrug*

☐ Peregrine Falcon *Falco peregrinus*

☐ Barbary Falcon *Falco pelegrinoides*

☑ Chukar *Alectoris chukar*, 90

☑ Sand Partridge *Ammoperdix heyi*, 89, 93

☐ Black Francolin *Francolinus francolinus*

☑ Grey Francolin *Francolinus pondicerianus*, 63, 64

☐ Quail *Coturnix coturnix*

☐ Water Rail *Rallus aquaticus*

☐ Spotted Crake *Porzana porzana*

☐ Little Crake *Porzana parva*

☐ Baillon's Crake *Porzana pusilla*

☐ Corncrake *Crex crex*

☐ Moorhen *Gallinula chloropus*

☐ Purple Gallinule *Porphyrio porphyrio*

☑ Coot *Fulica atra*, 39, 43

☐ Common Crane *Grus grus*

☐ Demoiselle Crane *Anthropoides virgo*

☑ Houbara Bustard *Chlamydotis undulata*, 83

☑ Oystercatcher *Haematopus ostralegus*, 26

☑ Black-winged Stilt *Himantopus himantopus*, 42, 44

☐ Avocet *Recurvirostra avosetta*

☑ Crab Plover *Dromas ardeola*, 28, 29, 30

☑ Stone Curlew *Burhinus oedicnemus*, 83

☑ Cream-coloured Courser *Cursorius cursor*, 83

☐ Collared Pratincole *Glareola pratincola*

☐ Black-winged Pratincole *Glareola nordmanni*

☐ Little Pratincole *Glareola lactea*

☑ Little Ringed Plover *Charadrius dubius*, 32, 33

☑ Ringed Plover *Charadrius hiaticula*, 32, 33

☑ Kentish Plover *Charadrius alexandrinus*, 32, 33

☑ Lesser Sand Plover *Charadrius mongolus*, 33

☑ Greater Sand Plover *Charadrius leschenaultii*, 33

☑ Caspian Plover *Charadrius asiaticus*, 31, 33

☑ Dotterel *Charadrius morinellus*, 33

☐ Pacific Golden Plover *Pluvialis fulva*

☑ Grey Plover *Pluvialis squatarola*, 32

☑ Red-wattled Lapwing *Hoplopterus indicus*, 90, 92

☐ Sociable Plover *Chettusia gregaria*

☐ White-tailed Plover *Chettusia leucura*

☑ Lapwing *Vanellus vanellus*, 43, 80

☐ Great Knot *Calidris tenuirostris*

☐ Knot *Calidris canutus*

☐ Sanderling *Calidris alba*

☑ Long-toed Stint *Calidris subminuta*, 42

☑ Little Stint *Calidris minuta*, 42

☑ Temminck's Stint *Calidris temminckii*, 42

☑ Curlew Sandpiper *Calidris ferruginea*, 26, 28, 31

☑ Dunlin *Calidris alpina*, 26, 28, 31

☑ Broad-billed Sandpiper *Limicola falcinellus*, 42

☑ Ruff *Philomachus pugnax*, 43, 44

☐ Jack Snipe *Lymnocryptes minimus*

☑ Common Snipe *Gallinago gallinago*, 43, 44

☐ Great Snipe *Gallinago media*

☐ Pintail Snipe *Gallinago stenura*

☐ Woodcock *Scolopax rusticola*

☑ Black-tailed Godwit *Limosa limosa*, 25, 39

☑ Bar-tailed Godwit *Limosa lapponica*, 21, 25, 39

☑ Whimbrel *Numenius phaeopus*, 25, 26

☑ Curlew *Numenius arquata*, 25, 26

☑ Spotted Redshank *Tringa erythropus*, 26

☑ Redshank *Tringa totanus*, 26

☑ Marsh Sandpiper *Tringa stagnatilis*, 42

☑ Greenshank *Tringa nebularia*, 26, 27

☑ Green Sandpiper *Tringa ochropus*, 42, 43, 90

☑ Wood Sandpiper *Tringa glareola*, 42, 43, 90

☑ Terek Sandpiper *Xenus cinereus*, 42, 45

☑ Common Sandpiper *Actitis hypoleucos*, 42, 43

☐ Turnstone *Arenaria interpres*

☐ Red-necked Phalarope *Phalaropus lobatus*

☐ Grey Phalarope *Phalaropus fulicariu*

☑ Pomarine Skua *Stercorarius pomarinus*, 23

☑ Arctic Skua *Stercorarius parasiticus*, 23, 31

☐ Long-tailed Skua *Stercorarius longicaudus*

☐ Great Skua *Stercorarius skua*

☑ Sooty Gull *Larus hemprichii*, 29

☑ Great Black-headed Gull *Larus ichthyaetus*, 29, 30, 32

☐ Sabine's Gull *Larus sabini*

☑ Black-headed Gull *Larus ridibundus*, 32, 59

☐ Brown-headed Gull *Larus brunnicephalus*

☑ Slender-billed Gull *Larus genei*, 32

☐ Common Gull *Larus canus*

CHECKLIST

☐ White Wagtail *Motacilla alba*, 57, 58, 80

☐ White-cheeked Bulbul
  Pycnonotus leucogenys, 53, 54, 90, 91

☐ Yellow-vented Bulbul *Pycnonotus xanthopygos*, 90, 91

☐ Red-whiskered Bulbul *Pycnonotus jocosus*

☐ Red-vented Bulbul *Pycnonotus cafer*, 54

☐ Hypocolius *Hypocolius ampelinus*

☐ Rufous Bush Chat *Cercotrichas galactotes*, 64, 65

☐ Robin *Erithacus rubecula*

☐ Thrush Nightingale *Luscinia luscinia*

☐ Nightingale *Luscinia megarhynchos*, 64

☐ Bluethroat *Luscinia svecica*

☐ White-throated Robin *Irania gutturalis*

☐ Eversmann's Redstart *Phoenicurus erythronotus*

☐ Black Redstart *Phoenicurus ochruros*, 55, 56

☐ Redstart *Phoenicurus phoenicurus*, 55, 56

☐ Whinchat *Saxicola rubetra*, 68

☐ Stonechat *Saxicola torquata*, 68

☐ Isabelline Wheatear *Oenanthe isabellina*, 69, 70

☐ Northern Wheatear *Oenanthe oenanthe*, 14, 69

☐ Pied Wheatear *Oenanthe pleschanka*, 69, 94

☐ Black-eared Wheatear *Oenanthe hispanica*, 15

☐ Desert Wheatear *Oenanthe deserti*, 69, 70

☐ Finsch's Wheatear *Oenanthe finschii*

☐ Red-tailed Wheatear *Oenanthe xanthoprymna*, 92, 94

☐ Eastern Pied Wheatear *Oenanthe picata*, 94, 95

☐ Mourning Wheatear *Oenanthe lugens*

☐ Hooded Wheatear *Oenanthe monacha*, 69, 88, 89

☐ Hume's Wheatear *Oenanthe alboniger*, 88, 94, 95

☐ White-crowned Black Wheatear *Oenanthe leucopyga*

☐ Rock Thrush *Monticola saxatilis*, 13, 15, 94

☐ Blue Rock Thrush *Monticola solitarius*, 93, 94

☐ Ring Ouzel *Turdus torquatus*

☐ Blackbird *Turdus merula*

☐ Eye-browed Thrush *Turdus obscurus*, 79

☐ Black-throated Thrush *Turdus ruficollis*

☐ Fieldfare *Turdus pilaris*

☐ Song Thrush *Turdus philomelos*

☐ Redwing *Turdus iliacus*

☐ Mistle Thrush *Turdus viscivorus*

☐ Graceful Warbler *Prinia gracilis*, 71

☐ Scrub Warbler *Scotocerca inquieta*

☐ Grasshopper Warbler *Locustella naevia*

☐ Savi's Warbler *Locustella luscinioides*

☐ Moustached Warbler *Acrocephalus melanopogon*

☐ Sedge Warbler *Acrocephalus schoenobaenus*

☐ Marsh Warbler *Acrocephalus palustris*

☐ Reed Warbler *Acrocephalus scirpaceus*, 8, 11

☐ Clamorous Reed Warbler
  Acrocephalus stentoreus, 46

☐ Great Reed Warbler *Acrocephalus arundinaceus*

☐ Olivaceous Warbler *Hippolais pallida*, 72, 73

☐ Booted Warbler *Hippolais caligata*

☐ Upcher's Warbler *Hippolais languida*, 11

☐ Icterine Warbler *Hippolais icterina*

☐ Ménétries' Warbler *Sylvia mystacea*, 10, 11

☐ Desert Warbler *Sylvia nana*

☐ Orphean Warbler *Sylvia hortensis*

☐ Barred Warbler *Sylvia nisoria*, 11

☐ Lesser Whitethroat *Sylvia curruca*, 11

☐ Desert Lesser Whitethroat *Sylvia minula*

☐ Hume's Lesser Whitethroat *Sylvia althaea*

☐ Common Whitethroat *Sylvia communis*

☐ Garden Warbler *Sylvia borin*

☐ Blackcap *Sylvia atricapilla*

☐ Yellow-browed Warbler *Phylloscopus inornatus*

☐ Dusky Warbler *Phylloscopus fuscatus*

☐ Bonelli's Warbler *Phylloscopus bonelli*

☐ Wood Warbler *Phylloscopus sibilatrix*

☐ Plain Leaf Warbler *Phylloscopus neglectus*

☐ Chiffchaff *Phylloscopus collybita*, 56, 80

☐ Willow Warbler *Phylloscopus trochilus*, 11, 56

☐ Blue-and-white Flycatcher *Muscicapa cyanomelana*

☐ Spotted Flycatcher *Muscicapa striata*, 55

☐ Red-breasted Flycatcher *Ficedula parva*, 55

☐ Semi-collared Flycatcher *Ficedula semitorquata*, 55

☐ Pied Flycatcher *Ficedula hypoleuca*

☐ Arabian Babbler *Turdoides squamiceps*, 90, 91

☐ Purple Sunbird *Nectarinia asiatica*, 61, 66

☐ Golden Oriole *Oriolus oriolus*, 56

☐ Isabelline Shrike *Lanius isabellinus*, 52, 54, 80

☐ Red-backed Shrike *Lanius collurio*, 6, 9

☐ Bay-backed Shrike *Lanius vittatus*

☐ Lesser Grey Shrike *Lanius minor*, 9, 84

☐ Great Grey Shrike *Lanius excubitor*, 9, 84, 85

☐ Woodchat Shrike *Lanius senator*, 9, 10

☐ Masked Shrike *Lanius nubicus*, 52, 55

☐ Black Drongo *Dicrurus macrocercus*

CHECKLIST

▨ Indicates birds mentioned in this book, together with the pages on which they appear.

BIBLIOGRAPHY

For those who may wish to read more about the birds of the region, we suggest the following books:

THE BIRDS OF OMAN
by Michael Gallagher and Martin Woodcock
Quartet Books,
ISBN 07043 2216 1

The most appropriate field guide for the area with good descriptions and beautiful illustrations of practically all the birds which occur in the region. Bulky, and difficult to obtain these days.

THE BIRDS OF THE UNITED ARAB EMIRATES
by Colin Richardson
Hobby Publications,
ISBN 1 872839 00 2

This book, with up-to-date information on status and distribution of the birds of the UAE, will appeal to the accomplished birder. It contains useful information on the best birding sites.

**THE BIRDS OF BRITAIN AND EUROPE
WITH NORTH AFRICA AND THE MIDDLE EAST**
by Heinzel, Parslow and Fitter
Collins,
ISBN 0 00 219210 1

One of the best old standard pocket field guides; inexpensive and serves the purposes of most beginners. Covering a wide geographical area, the illustrations and text are necessarily brief.

NATURAL HISTORY AND BIRD GROUP ADDRESSES FOR THE AREA:–

Emirates Natural History Group
PO Box 2380, Abu Dhabi, UAE

Dubai Natural History Group
PO Box 9234, Dubai, UAE

Emirates Bird Group
c/o Colin Richardson,
PO Box 2825, Dubai, UAE

Qatar Natural History Group
c/o Robert Nation
ICS Dept, QGPC
PO Box 3212, Doha, Qatar

Oman Bird Group
c/o The Natural History Museum
PO Box 668, Muscat, Oman

Bahrain Natural History Society
PO Box 1858, Bahrain

AUTHORS

Adrian Chapman's interest in bird-watching began as a child in his native Yorkshire, and he visited most of the birding hot spots of northern England and Scotland in his teens. He was an assistant leader on several expeditions to Iceland, Shetland and Norway to study birds.

Following an apprenticeship in engineering he joined the Merchant Navy and watched seabirds throughout the world's oceans. Coming ashore after 16 years of seafaring he works as a Ship and Engineering Surveyor for Lloyds Register of Shipping. He spent 12 years in the UAE. Initially located in Dubai, he was active in helping to establish the Dubai Natural History Group and provided many of the original bird records before moving to Abu Dhabi.

Dave Robinson was born in Northumberland and had a keen childhood interest in natural history. As an Engineer working in the oil industry he first ventured overseas to Libya where the excellent bird-watching opportunities re-awakened his interest in the subject. A transfer to the jungles of Malaysia increased his fascination and added the desire to not only identify his findings but to record them on film.

On relocating to Abu Dhabi he met up with Adrian and the pair set out to explore the UAE and its borders over the next four to five years. They travelled extensively, recording their findings including several firsts for the region. In the later years they began to collect photographs of the birds, and the idea for this book emerged.

Adrian is currently in Hong Kong where he reports excellent bird-watching opportunities and Dave is returning to his native Northumberland where he plans to re-explore and photograph the birds of his youth.

ACKNOWLEDGEMENTS

First and foremost we would like to thank all our friends and acquaintances in the UAE who have wittingly or otherwise helped or encouraged us in both confirming and creating the need for this book. Our particular thanks go to our bird-watching colleagues, the 'girls', Jenny and Linda; the Richardsons, Colin and Bob; Bish Brown; Len Reaney; Rob and Penny Quested; and Peter Hellyer; all of whom will have heard the text many times before.

Thanks also to Maarten Verhage who took us offshore and provided the missing photograph, and to Ghassan Ghussain who arranged to let us visit some of the islands and always demonstrated that genuine Arab hospitality you hear about.

We especially thank our families — the kids, Renée and Lara, and Jake and Emma, who may have seen more of the birds than they wished, camped in some odd locations and had to endure long minutes of inactivity and silence in the pursuit of a photograph; Veronica who is no lover of the great outdoors, but survived it, and Moira, a constant companion, driver, film loader and everything else that was required.

And finally we would like to express our gratitude to Exxon, whose sponsorship has made possible the publication of this book.

Arabian Profiles
edited by Ian Fairservice
and Chuck Grieve

Land of the Emirates
by Shirley Kay

Enchanting Oman
by Shirley Kay

Bahrain — Island Heritage
by Shirley Kay

Dubai — Gateway to the Gulf
edited by Ian Fairservice

Abu Dhabi — Garden City
of the Gulf
by Peter Hellyer
and Ian Fairservice

Fujairah — An Arabian Jewel
by Peter Hellyer

Portrait of Ras Al Khaimah
by Shirley Kay

Sharjah — Heritage and Progress
by Shirley Kay

Architectural Heritage
of the Gulf
by Shirley Kay
and Dariush Zandi

Emirates Archaeological Heritage
by Shirley Kay

Seafarers of the Gulf
by Shirley Kay

Gulf Landscapes
by Elizabeth Collas
and Andrew Taylor

Birds of Southern Arabia
by Dave Robinson
and Adrian Chapman

Mammals of the Southern Gulf
by Christian Gross

The Living Desert
by Marycke Jongbloed

Seashells of Southern Arabia
by Donald and Eloise Bosch

The Living Seas
by Frances Dipper
and Tony Woodward

Sketchbook Arabia
by Margaret Henderson

The Thesiger Collection
a catalogue of unique photographs
by Wilfred Thesiger

Thesiger's Return
by Peter Clark
Black and white photography
by Wilfred Thesiger

Juha — Last of the Errant Knights
by Mustapha Kamal,
translated by Jack Briggs

Fun in the Emirates
by Aisha Bowers
and Leslie P. Engelland

Mother Without a Mask
by Patricia Holton

Library boxes and boxed sets
are also available

Arabian Albums
Dubai
An Arabian Album
by Ronald Codrai

Abu Dhabi
An Arabian Album
by Ronald Codrai

Premier Editions
A Day Above Oman
by John Nowell

Land of the Emirates
by Shirley Kay

Enchanting Oman
by Shirley Kay

Dubai — Gateway to the Gulf
edited by Ian Fairservice

Abu Dhabi — Garden City
of the Gulf
edited by Ian Fairservice
and Peter Hellyer

Arabian Heritage Guides
Snorkelling and
Diving in Oman
by Rod Salm and Robert Baldwin

The Green Guide
to the Emirates
by Marycke Jongbloed

Off-Road in the Emirates
by Dariush Zandi

Off-Road in Oman
by Heiner Klein
and Rebecca Brickson

MOTIVATE
PUBLISHING